# Nurturing Social and Emotional Development

A programme of work for KS2 and KS3 pupils
By
Tina Rae, Beth Hodgson & Katherine McKenna

www.nurturegroups.org

# CONTENTS

Page No.

## Part 1

| | |
|---|---|
| Forewords | 1 |
| About the authors | 3 |
| Introduction | 5 |
| References | 19 |
| Introductory PowerPoint – Training session for staff | 22 |

## Part 2 - The Programme

| | |
|---|---|
| 1 Self-awareness | 35 |
| 2 Managing feelings | 58 |
| 3 Motivation | 80 |
| 4 Empathy | 102 |
| 5 Social skills | 124 |

## Part 3 - Appendices

| | |
|---|---|
| Setting up the Grange Nurture Group – a history in words and pictures | 147 |
| Case studies | 151 |
| The pre and post checklist | 156 |
| Information sheet for staff and parents | 159 |

Copyright of the Nurture Group Network 2011

# Part 1

- **Forewords**

- **About the authors**

- **Introduction**

- **References**

- **Introductory PowerPoint - Training Session for Staff**

# Foreword

I am pleased to write a foreword to this important publication which is the result of a special school recognising that the inclusive, targeted and systematic approach offered in a Nurture Group would help their pupils when early life experiences were stopping them accessing education. It tells the story of the setting up of one group and provides an interesting, comprehensive and developmentally progressive set of activities and lesson plans based on the SEAL domains.

The Nurture Group Network has been delighted to help produce and fund the publication as it is definitely not only for special schools but also useful for mainstream practitioners as well as those working with pupils in special units, pupil referral units or with any young person who struggles with their emotions when having to turn take, follow instructions, think of others, concentrate or wait to share support workers' time and efforts. Most people think of lack of employment as being the long term effect of not engaging in education but they should also think of both mental and physical health together with the possibility of being drawn into anti-social and delinquent behaviours.

Led by the inspirational Dr Tina Rae, Steve, Beth and Katherine have not only rearranged rooms and timetables but also set up lesson plans and activities to use to support these pupils. Their secure base and staff offer unconditional warmth and acceptance. Together with the activities, they allow the pupils to engage in the process of learning and develop the confidence that enables them to find their place in the wider school and life communities.

In this work, key early learning experiences and developmentally appropriate activities provide a fun way to engage pupils and change their perception of their own ability, their relationships with others and their learning capacity.

*Marian Evans*
Chair Board of Trustees
The Nurture Group Network

# Foreword

As Principal of the Grange school, I am delighted to have been directly involved in developing our whole school approach to nurturing the young people in our care, whilst also promoting and developing our Nurture base and our social, emotional and behavioural skills curriculum.

In our special context, we have always recognised how emotional well-being underpins learning and the tensions between the achievement culture and the nurturing culture. As a result, we have aimed to ensure high quality relationships between staff and pupils and planned the curriculum based on an understanding of each student's needs – both emotional and cognitive. We know that many of the young people referred to us may have displayed insecure early attachments and encountered difficulties which will have impacted upon the development of both social and emotional skills and their learning. Our therapeutic context and our commitment to nurturing principles is key to our success in ensuring the well being and on-going development of our young people in all areas. With the support of Dr Tina Rae we have been able to systematically translate these into practice in the creation of our nurturing provision and curriculum.

Consequently, I do hope that this publication will inspire colleagues to further develop their practice in this area whilst also provide them with a range of relevant and wholly practical resources which have been successfully trialled at the Grange.

I am proud to maintain and further develop my commitment to an approach which, in the words of Tony Cline (2009) is, 'inclusive, targeted, systematic and intellectually coherent, with a well-defined curriculum and clear programme for parental involvement'. I am also proud to have been able to support and facilitate my staff team, working in partnership with Dr Tina Rae, in developing this highly practical, inclusive and timely resource.

*Steve Watt*
Principal
The Grange school
June 2011

# Dr Tina Rae

BA(hons) PGCE MA(Ed) Msc RSADipSpLD DipPsych ALCM Doc App Ch Ed Psy
HPC registered Educational Psychologist,
**Author and Educational Consultant**

Dr Tina Rae is a Consultant Educational Psychologist and has a wealth of experience in working therapeutically with children and young people and their parents/carers. She is a registered member of the Health Professions Council and a full member of the British Psychological Society. She is currently working as a Consultant EP and as an Academic and professional tutor on the Doctoral training course for Educational Psychologists in the department of Psychology at the University of East London.

Tina has written extensively for Lucky Duck Publishing, Sage publications, Folens Publications, Paul Chapman Publications and for Optimus Education on topics including social and emotional skills development, anger management, grief, loss and bereavement, critical incidents, emotional literacy, self harm and suicide, and the use of therapeutic interventions with children and young people. Tina contributes to conferences and training courses across the country. She is a member of the SEBDA council and a co-opted member of the ENGAGE national committee.

# Katherine McKenna

Katherine McKenna is currently teaching at The Grange school and has been working in both a therapeutic and educational capacity with young people for the last 9 years and has also been working as a class teacher for 4 years.

The children being referred were also increasingly displaying a range of attachment difficulties and were clearly in need of a nurturing environment to ease them back into the 'standard' ideal of a classroom and the learning context. Along with her colleague and mentor Beth Hodgson, Katherine wanted to provide a nurturing environment. She subsequently did some research and discovered that 'nurture' and the notion of 'Nurture Groups' were becoming increasingly popular in educational settings. They trialled some 'nurturing' approaches and systems and this immediately produced some more positive results. So, they then decided to expand their ideas and began to write a nurturing curriculum for the lower school in order to further build upon the creation of their nurture classroom and soft room. This is when Dr. Tina Rae became involved. Everything came together in terms of setting up the Nurture Room and with this publication being one of the direct results of this collaboration.

Katherine is delighted to be involved in this project and have the opportunity to use her experience in supporting young children with social, behavioural and emotional needs in this way. She is committed to delivering a curriculum which ensures the well being and development of vulnerable youngsters and remains a highly valued member of the staff team at the Grange.

# Mrs. Beth Hodgson

Beth Hodgson has a BeD Hons degree, specialising in Primary School. She has an additional NPQH qualification. She taught in various Primary Schools and began to realise her expertise lay with children with special educational needs, especially those with behaviour difficulties. She has taught at The Grange School for four and a half years and became the Head and SENCo of the Lower School a year after joining.

Soon after joining the school Beth created a new curriculum for the whole of Lower School. This was awarded the standard of 'outstanding' in the 2009 OFSTED report.

Beth is excited and honoured to be involved in a project that has developed from a small idea into a shared venture that is making a positive difference in developing the needs of young children with social, emotional and behavioural difficulties.

# Introduction

This book aims to provide staff in both mainstream and special contexts with resources to develop and deliver a programme to support the development of children's social, emotional and behavioural skills. It is based upon nurturing principles and promotes the use of nurture groups in schools, providing not only the necessary resources to set up and run such an intervention but also a comprehensive programme of social skills activities and resources which aims to build upon the five SEAL domains. The design and content of the programme clearly takes into account the needs of children who, to varying degrees, have been unable to access the basic and essential learning that is usually a direct result of close, twisting bonds with care-givers in the early years. The difficulties they experience are generally related to stress experienced by parents/carers which impaired the early nurturing process and consequently led to impairments in both cognitive and emotional development.

The Steer Report on behaviour in schools, Learning Behaviour: Lessons learned (DCSF, 2009) identified nurture groups as being an important resource in terms of improving children's behaviour. The approach and rationale is underpinned by psychological theory and evidence whilst also being cost-effective and accessible to staff in schools and early years settings.

Such evidence, alongside that from both early years and secondary settings (Bennathan and Rose, 2008) provided us with our rationale and impetus to develop this programme and set up our nurture provision within the context of The Grange School.

# Our Context

The Grange Therapeutic School is a 38 week residential school providing weekly boarding for boys aged 8-16 who have a statement of Social, Emotional Behavioural Difficulties. The School also has a number of day pupils. Within the Lower School the majority of the boys are day pupils. Students are referred to the school from local authorities throughout England.

At the core of its success is the high quality of relationships between staff and pupils, based on an understanding of each boy's needs. The school provides a safe and healthy environment from which pupils can access the high quality of teaching on offer.

The school offers a wide curriculum and an abundance of extra-curricular activities including a range of outdoor pursuits, which is successful in re-engaging reluctant learners.

Many of the children referred to the school will display insecure attachments and will have experienced traumatic events in their early years. The latter will have impacted negatively upon the development of social and emotional skills and negative behaviour patterns may have prevented age appropriate achievements.

At the Grange we offer a range of therapeutic interventions across all key stages. Within the Lower School we have also recognised the need to intervene at the earliest opportunity in terms of nurturing the well being of our young students. This has led to the development of a nurture base, a curriculum delivered via nurturing principles and the development of a social and emotional skills programme for the Lower School.

It is this curriculum which provides a comprehensive programme for supporting the development of our children's social and emotional skills within a nurturing framework. The development and roll-out of the SEAL curriculum and approaches (DFES) is currently on-going across all key stages and overall awareness of the importance of developing these skills has been raised significantly in recent years. It now appears to be more commonly accepted that basic social skills and the development of an emotional vocabulary are essential pre-requisites for learning and well being as a whole. Children need these skills if they are to develop appropriately and function effectively within both the social and learning contexts. The development of such skills is also much more likely to ensure academic success and this 'emotional intelligence' is probably the most powerful predictor of future life success (Goleman 1995).

## The Need for Social Skills Training

Given the fact that social skills are vital for a child's future development, it seems logical to ensure that such skills are taught within our school curriculum. The early years are when young children begin to develop these skills – learning to co-operate, take turns and solve the social problems that they are likely to encounter on a daily basis. Children need to learn how to wait their turn, share, resolve conflicts, cope effectively with anger, respond assertively in some contexts and gain confidence in social situations. If these skills are not learnt in the early years there will naturally be an impact upon overall development. As stated earlier, some children will develop these skills more easily than others – particularly those raised in secure, emotionally literate contexts. Clearly the profile of some students is such that they have not been nurtured within such contexts and have consequently not developed appropriately secure attachments. This has resulted in significant gaps in social, emotional and cognitive learning.

Children need to progress through a series of developmental stages, one of which needs to involve exploratory play. Without this kind of natural progression they will fail to develop the social and emotional skills necessary to access an age appropriate curriculum. The majority of our children have not had access to such environments and for such children, additional teaching to learn to interact socially, ask for help and support, assert themselves and manage anxiety and stress will be necessary. They also need to be provided with opportunities to learn these skills through play as many of them will clearly have missed out on this particular stage and consequently find it difficult to interact appropriately and engage in learning tasks. Those who are aggressive or impulsive will also require such additional support in order to learn how to wait their turn, share, resolve conflicts, empathise with others, cope with strong feelings such as anger and to develop assertive as opposed to aggressive behaviours and responses. Children with Asperger's Syndrome or Autism will also require additional support in order to develop basic social skills such as making eye contact, recognising emotions and developing empathy. It is hoped that this scheme of work will go some way to providing practitioners with the practical resources to teach these skills in an engaging and interactive manner – in both the special and mainstream context.

## The Vicious Cycle

Children who present as aggressive – both physically and verbally – tend to be rejected by their peers and those who present as withdrawn may often be left out of activities and isolated and ignored. This can lead to a vicious cycle in which these children consequently do not interact as much as others in their peer group. They subsequently have fewer opportunities to learn, practice and develop the basic social skills that they need in order to become socially integrated. Such children will tend to fall behind socially and the gap between them and others in their peer group may well increase to a significant level. This is particularly distressing given the fact that these early years are so crucial in terms of social and emotional development. There is evidence to suggest that the quality of children's peer adjustment in the primary phase and their peer status amongst new classmates (Ladd 1981). Mize and Ladd (1990) also identified how interventions with pre-school children were successful in teaching pro-social skills, in reducing inappropriate/negative behaviours (Gresham and Nagle, 1980) and in increasing the social interaction of children labelled as withdrawn or over anxious (Evers and Schwartz, 1973).

## Social Skills Intervention

Much of the research literature to both evaluate and support the delivery of social skills interventions of this nature has outlined a general agreement that a) the arrangement can produce important changes in identified social behaviours and that b) training in specific social skills can be accomplished by means of such procedures as modelling, behavioural rehearsal, feedback and practice. Various reviews of the relevant literature support these conclusions (Cartledge & Milburn, 1980; Hops & Greenwood, 1981; Van Hasselt et al (1979) made the point that when a child lacks specific social skills that are needed to be effective in social situations, it is not appropriate to simply apply reinforcing contingencies. Rather, a combination of instruction in the missing skills with such contingencies is needed.

## Reinforcement and Generalisation in Everyday Situations

The fact that young children learn best through modelling and practice is not in dispute (Evers & Schwartz, 1973). However, a frequently noted problem is the generalisation of such newly trained skills to significant environments (Berter, Gross & Drabman, 1982; Cooke & Apolloni, 1976; La Greca & Santogrossi, 1980). This is a particular problem if/when the training is conducted away from the child's natural environment. In such instances, careful attention needs to be paid to identifying ways to enhance generalisation and incorporating these into any intervention plan. In our context, we have consequently decided to adopt nurturing principles and utilise a range of key strategies and techniques from this approach in order to effectively deliver an appropriate scheme of work to our children from Lower KS2 to Lower KS3.

## Nurture Groups

Nurture groups were developed in 1969 in inner London as a response to the large number of children presenting to psychological services with severe social, emotional and behavioural needs on entering school. Marjory Boxall, an Educational Psychologist, recognised the difficulties presented by this group of children and the ways in which these were directly related to impoverished early nurturing. This resulted in many of the children being unable to form trusting relationships with adults or to respond appropriately to other children. In effect, they were simply not ready to meet the social and intellectual demands of school life. For Boxall the main aim of the nurture group intervention was therefore to 'create the world of earliest childhood; building the basic and essential learning experiences normally gained in the first three years of life and enable children to fully meet their potential in mainstream schools'. (Boxall, 2002).

## Theoretical Underpinning

Pupa et al (2001) suggested that the guiding theory of nurture groups was that children who exhibited emotional and behavioural difficulties were very often experiencing emotions and exhibiting behaviours that developmentally were appropriate for children of a younger chronological age.

For Boxall (2002) the focus of a nurture group should therefore be building early attachments and the recreation of early care of child interactions.

## What is a Nurture Group in a Mainstream Context?

The guiding principles of any nurture group are as follows:
1. Children's learning is understood developmentally
2. the nurture group class offers a secure base
3. Nurture is important for self-esteem
4. Language is a vital means of communication
5. All behaviour is communication
6. Transition is important in children's lives

In effect a nurture group is an inclusive early intervention for the development of social, emotional and behavioural difficulties within a mainstream setting. It is a provision in which the day is one of carefully structured routines providing a balance of learning, teaching, affection and structure within a homelike environment. It is also a group in which children are placed, not due to their limitations with regards to ability, but simply because they have missed out on early experiences that promote good development particularly in the areas of social, emotional and behavioural skills.

Nurture groups offer a context and a model of relationships to children who have been missing or who have insufficiently internalised essential early learning experiences. They are generally a within-school resource staffed by two adults for up to 10 children and offer short or medium placements where the children attend regularly usually returning fully to their mainstream classroom within two-four terms. Nurture groups do not in any sense stigmatise the children who attend since the intervention is planned as part of a whole school approach to supporting children. In fact the children generally have strong links with their mainstream class, for example registering there in the morning, attending selective activities and spending great time in lunchtimes with their classroom peer group.

The nurture group takes place within the nurture room which aims to provide a secure, predictable environment to meet the different needs of each child. There is a strong focus on supporting positive emotional and social growth and cognitive development at the level of the individual child by responding to each child in a developmentally appropriate way.

## Snack Time

Snack time is an essential part of the nurture group routine and is rich in communication and language.

Misconception and prejudice leaves many nurture group practitioners in the position of explaining snack time is not a substitute for breakfast club but a vital part of the nurture curriculum. Clear boundaries and structure allow each child to contribute.

It is an opportunity to share information or reflect on work undertaken as well as talking about families and friends. This activity may seem enjoyable and relaxing but the pupils have to work very hard to maintain the social interaction expected of them during this time. With fewer and fewer families sitting to a food sharing routine, snack time provides opportunities for making acceptable choices, voicing them in an appropriate manner, sharing and taking the needs of others into account. Hand (2002) states that family meals allow opportunities to bond, plan, connect and learn from one another. Snack time is an opportunity to foster warmth, security and a feeling of belonging.

It is vital that both members of staff sit and eat with the children. Making the food then standing watching the children eat would distance the children from the adults and miss the opportunity for developing trusting bonds. The chores involved to make this successful should be distributed and on a rota displayed in the area for all to share.

## Setting up our Nurture Group Room(s) / Approach at The Grange

At Lower School, some of our children evidently fall into this group who have generally missed out on early learning experiences and the opportunities to form secure attachments with significant adults. This has resulted in a wide range of social, emotional and behavioural difficulties which we feel can now be most appropriately nurtured within this kind of nurturing context. All children will have access to the appropriate national curriculum but this will be delivered within a context that simultaneously supports the development of social and emotional skills and recognises and meets the needs of young children who are functioning at a lower level (both socially and academically) than would normally be expected at their current chronological age.

Our current rooms are intended as educational settings but include elements of a secure and supportive home alongside the normal classroom furniture. There are comfortable chairs and sofas, a cooking area and a large mirror. The rooms have four or five areas: a kitchen area, a dining area, a role play area and a quiet area. All these areas are appropriately resourced with classic features of the early years classroom while supplementary resources may also include the following:

- A small writing or book making corner
- A work area
- A listening station which is valuable when children want to listen to story tapes or simply record their own stories, thoughts and feelings and share them later if they so desire
- Sand and water areas
- Train sets and play bricks
- A quiet 'cocoon' area for children who need to curl up and be apart from the rest of the group at any point during the sessions
- A range of resources and activities to promote turn taking and social skills in general which are available generally (these can be rotated from time to time so that all children are not overwhelmed by choice)
- Display boards for children's work and also for information, targets and timetabling

## The Timetable

We use this curriculum in nurture group sessions which are approximately two hours in length and it is clearly more practical, in terms of the school timetable, to ensure that times remain consistent throughout the year. The first half hour of the session is when the children engage in free play; they can access a range of activities at this time and it is an ideal opportunity for staff to observe the children's learning and development of social and emotional skills. Table top and floor activities can be set up to cover each area of learning. The second 45 minutes of the session is when the children engage in group time. One member of the staff will lead the group whilst the other becomes a member of the group providing a role model for the children. Activities in this session may be developed on the following:

- days of the week
- weather
- finding name cards
- choosing a special helper
- playing a short game linked to social skills development
- playing the 'bag' game

The next 30 minutes is for snack time. This is when a special helper helps prepare and serve the snack and drinks to the peer group. During this time both the adults and the children sit down together at the table; this enables the adults to model social conversation and engage in any problem solving regarding a current issue that may have arisen within the group. The next part of the session involves focused teaching. This is when one member of staff will carry out focused teaching tasks with individual children. Each child will try to complete the task during this time, either in a one to one or a small group context. This enables the other member of staff to interact with other children in their play whilst these activities are being implemented.

The final part of the nurture group session is that of story time where one member of the staff reads a story to the group as a whole while the other member of staff becomes part of the group once again. This enables them to model appropriate behaviour, listening skills etc and also support the children's enjoyment, learning and development of language skills.

## Nurture Group Timetable in the Specialist Setting

At The Grange School all staff are encouraged to adopt nurturing principles ensuring that each curriculum area presents tasks in a practical and engaging way with copious opportunities to develop both social and emotional skills through play based and creative approaches.

Currently children have access to a nurture room which is set up in the traditional way as described earlier. They also have access to a bespoke kitchen area and dining room which clearly provide many opportunities to practise appropriate social skills whilst also developing academic skills in a range of subject areas e.g. numeracy, literacy.

The timetable is constructed to ensure a balance between academic tasks and opportunities to have social and emotional skills reinforced on a daily basis. Children access teaching from both Lower School and Upper School staff. The latter teach lessons in the following subjects: PE, music, art. DT and science. The 5x55min lessons currently available are differentiated so as to ensure a range of practical tasks and teaching and learning styles. There is a focus on 'learning through doing' and an awareness of children differing attention and learning capabilities i.e. a 10/20 min 'learning task' may then be followed by 10/20 min 'practical nurture task', or alternatively, personalised access to time in the formal nurture room as appropriate. At present this is arranged on an individual needs basis. For example, a child who is experiencing high levels of distress will generally have more focused and timetabled time in the nurture room.

This ultimately ensures that each child's programme is personalised and needs are met appropriately on an individual basis. The nurture room is not, in any sense, used as a reward for inappropriate behaviour. In essence, it provides a sanctuary for the more distressed child in which emotional needs can subsequently be addressed so that he can then proceed to access learning.

All children also access 20-30 min of group social skills activities on a daily basis. These form part 2 of this programme offering a comprehensive and adaptable set of resources to develop children's social and emotional skills. These are described in further detail with session plans for ease of delivery.

## Social Skills Activities

As stated earlier during the second 45 minutes of a traditional nurture group session the students engage in group time. This involves a range of activities including the 'bag' game and a range of Circle time, turn taking and games activities. Most of these will be familiar to the early years practitioner but the 'bag' game may be a fresh means of developing such skills and is frequently used within the Nurture Group context.

## The Bag Game

The Bag Game is a particularly useful means of developing both social and emotional skills alongside the language skills needed to engage in effective and appropriate communication. In each of the sessions we have included this activity as we feel that it is one of the easiest means of promoting and developing these skills and also it is generally seen as a 'fun' or 'game' activity by the majority of children and young people. There is clearly some work involved in terms of collecting the relevant resources for each session but we feel that this is entirely worthwhile and the fact that the resources, once collected can be used time and time again is also helpful for the teacher or facilitator. Also, this is a particularly powerful means of developing language skills which enables each child to begin at their own current level of competence. The skills can be built upon as the sessions proceed with the facilitator encouraging the use of more descriptive vocabulary and more content as they see fit.

A range of items which are suggested in the list below can be placed into a bag and this is then passed around the group during a circle time session. One item is picked out by an individual child and this then supports the development of a range of cognitive and language skills. Given the size of the group it is also possible for all members of the group to have a turn. Ideas for the bag game include the following:

### Emotion cards:
- guess the picture and explain the feeling
- find the pair
- make the face
- pass the emotion around the circle

### Colour/shape/animal badges:
- name badge/object
- swap with same/different

### Colour or shape bracelets:
- name
- swap with a partner

### Objects e.g. ball/car/train:
- roll to a named person
- adult/choose peer

### Object e.g. toy/puppet/snake/water cylinder:
- pass around circle
- in time to music
- talk about what it feels like
- talk about how it makes you feel

### Words/objects Chinese Whispers:
- pass the word/mime around the circle

### Objects selected e.g. numbers/ bear pictures/soft toy

Songs:
- identifying the song by guessing from the objects selected

### Nursery rhymes

Pictures:
- build up rhyme with pictures, words etc
- ordering/sequencing of pictures

### Magic wand:
- the wand "tells" the children what to do
- stand up/clap hands/click fingers
- swap with a partner
- say your name/age
- say your favourite food/toy/game/TV programme

### Magnifying glasses:
- to get everyone to say a positive comment about the person next to them
- "I can see you have a happy face"
- "I like your jumper…"
- "I like you because…"
- "You are my friend because …"
- "You are kind because…"

### Picture cards:
- Find the pair that
- Are heavy/light
- You eat/drink

### Chatterbox cards:
- Find the card that is big/small
- Point to your ear/Zoe's ear

Our current curriculum incorporates aspects of all the above activities alongside a range of social and emotional skills development tools selected form current appropriate publications. These are arranged under the 5 SEAL domains and provide an academic year's curriculum for the children. The lesson plans and notes for delivery can be accessed in part 2.

## The Circle Time Approach

It is evident that many of the activities adopt the use of Circle Time approaches and we would therefore strongly recommend that potential facilitators are aware of this approach and feel relatively confident in using it to foster social and emotional development and the self esteem of the young people in their care. Circle Time is essentially a speaking and listening process in which children and young people are encouraged to speak and listen individually, in pairs, and in smaller and larger groups. Through Circle Time, children learn how to communicate, how to speak confidently and coherently and how to actively listen to other people and how to respond to them – both verbally and non-verbally. These are all essential life skills which we know that these resources seek to foster and further devolop. As with the Bag Game, what is important to reinforce is the fact that this approach is essentially fun and enables children to develop their skills in a non judgemental and empathic context.

Alongside this approach, it is also important for the facilitator to continually develop language skills, listening and attention skills in every activity undertaken in the Nurture group.

### Top Tips for developing these skills include the following:

Always gain the child's attention
Try not to have to compete with other noise
Use the child's name
Be prepared to repeat instructions calmly
Reward compliance
Keep a sense of humour
Establish routines so that instruction giving is minimised
Check with the child that they have heard the instructions appropriately
Encourage the child not to talk when someone else is talking
Encourage and reward the completion of tasks and activities e.g. puzzles
Use activities to develop special listening skills e.g.
-listen to story tapes
-close your eyes and talk about sounds that you hear (inside and outside)
-make animal or every day noises for the child to identify

-make up a story with the child's name in it and ask the child to clap their hands when they hear it
-ask the child to study a set of objects that make sounds when manipulated. Encourage the child to close their eyes and identify each object as it is used
-play 'I spy' games
-go over and repeat old nursery rhymes and jingles

## The Boxall Profile

When including children into a nurture group there needs to be a systematic assessment in which appropriate diagnostic and evaluative instruments have been used. The Boxall Profile provides a framework for this structured observation of children in the classroom and consists of two sections: developmental profile and diagnostic profile. This assessment tool is developed as part of the nurture group approach to allow for a precise way of assessing the areas of strength and difficulty that children experience in order to then enable a focused and fanned intervention and also a means of measuring progress. Good practice would suggest that the Boxall Profile would not be used as a sole assessment tool but should be supported with other assessments measures and professional opinion and reflection.

We have consequently developed our own pre and post intervention check list specifically deigned to support the delivery and evaluation of the 50 session programme and to further aid the assessment undertaken using the Boxall Profile. This check list rates pupils against a series of statements which describe development in the following areas.

- School behaviours
- Management of feelings
- Friendship skills
- Social skills

The check lists are completed by the teacher or adult who knows the pupils best. Consultation with other staff members is then taken and this may also involve a multi agency meeting. Children's profiles are carefully considered and it usually the case that those that score low in these key areas will have more access to the nurture group context than those that do not. The check list can be updated on a termly basis and reveal progress in key areas. This will then enable for the personalised plan to be developed i.e. children may access a combination of the nurture group and standard curriculum input. However, it is important to remember that all our children in this special context will invariably require access to this resource alongside ongoing access to the daily group social sessions.

The pre and post student checklist can be found in appendix 3.

## Success Story

As reported in The Independent on 6th September 2007 today's heads and teachers understand better than their predecessors how emotional well-being underpins learning. They are also clearly having to cope with a rising number of young children with problems and additionally the Government's Educational Agenda is turning the spotlight on the power of early intervention and upon the needs of the individual child. As Jim Rose, the previous Director of the Nurture Group Network stated "for a time, there was something of a conflict between the achievement culture and the nurturing culture, but nurture groups have grown faster over the past five years. There are at least 1000 groups, and probably more, in primary schools – mostly 5-7 years olds in KS1, although they are spread right across the primary range – and there are now also about 100 in secondary schools".

It seems that the evidence of the success of this kind of intervention is now mounting. For example, in Glasgow which has 69 groups research published in 2007 revealed that they have had a significant impact, not only on attendance and behaviour, but also upon academic achievement. The Ofsted report on nurture groups published July 12th 2011 recognises that nurture groups run by well trained staff who ensure no curriculum element is missed make a huge impact on emotional and social development thereby enabling pupils to break down their barriers to learning and successfully access the curriculum.

For these reasons this intervention is strongly recommended as a practical and hugely successful tool for inclusion for our more vulnerable children and young people. Such an evidence base also provides the justification for adopting such an approach and utilising these guiding principles within our specialist context.

## Supporting SEAL – An Important Task

Our scheme of work is also intended to be consistent with whole school approaches to fostering the Social and Emotional Aspects of Learning (SEAL). As the latter approach and curriculum are currently being delivered within many schools across the country, it is perhaps appropriate to define and briefly outline this approach in order to subsequently highlight how this approach embeds many of the social and emotional skills taught.

The Guidance Booklet (DCFS 2007) defines SEAL as follows:

'SEAL is a comprehensive approach to promoting the social and emotional skills that underpin effective learning, positive behaviour, regular attendance, staff effectiveness and the emotional health and well-being of all who learn and work in schools. It proposes that the skills will be most effectively developed by pupils, and at the same time enhance the skills of staff, through:

- Using a whole-school approach to create the climate and conditions that implicitly promote the skills and allow these to be practised and consolidated;
- Direct and focused learning opportunities for whole classes and as part of focus group work;
- Using learning and teaching approaches that support pupils to learn social and emotional skills and consolidate those already learnt;
- Continuing professional development for the whole staff of a school'
(DCSF 2007 p.4)

The social and emotional skills taught and fostered through this nurture approach include those of making and sustaining positive relationships and understanding and managing oneself and ones emotions, thoughts and behaviours. When human beings develop such skills they are subsequently more able to understand and respond effectively to the behaviours and emotions of others. Once again, the DCSF guidance booklet is explicit regarding the positive outcomes for people who are successfully able to develop these skills. Such people are more likely to:

- 'Be effective and successful learners;
- Be self-motivated;
- Make and sustain friendships;
- Deal with and resolve conflict effectively and fairly;
- Solve problems with others or by themselves;
- Manage strong feelings such as frustration, anger and anxiety;
- Be able to promote calm and optimistic states that promote the achievement of goals;

- Recover from setbacks and persist in the face of difficulties;
- Work co-operatively;
- Recognise and stand up for their own rights and the rights of others;
- Understand and value differences and commonalities between people, respecting the right of others to have beliefs and values different from their own.'

(DCSF 2007 p.4-5)

# The Five Domains

The SEAL approach and curriculum aims to support the children's development of social and emotional skills and overall well-being. In order to allow for more systematic thinking about these skills, the authors categorise them into five broad headings in line with Daniel Goleman's 5 Domains (1995). These are as follows:

## 1. Self-awareness

This domain focuses upon self-knowledge and valuing of oneself. It also includes developing an understanding of how the individual thinks and feels. Individuals are able to identify and describe their beliefs, values and feelings and feel good about who they are. They are also able to identify strengths and weaknesses and consequently learn more effectively and engage in positive interactions with other people.

## 2. Managing Feelings

This domain focuses upon how individuals express emotions, cope with change and difficult and uncomfortable feelings. There is also a focus upon increasing and enhancing the positive feelings experienced and to develop strategies for expressing feelings in a positive way. Developing ways of coping with uncomfortable feelings should, in turn, aid concentration, the development of pro-social behaviours and co-operative and productive relationships.

## 3. Motivation

This domain focuses upon working towards goals and being more persistent, resilient and optimistic. When individuals are able to set themselves goals, work out strategies for reaching these goals and respond appropriately to any difficulties encountered, then the learning process will be more productive. Students who can approach learning situations in such a positive way are also able to maximise their ability to achieve their full potential.

## 4. Empathy

This domain focuses upon understanding how other people think and feel and provides the notions of valuing and respecting others. When individuals are truly able to understand, respect and value others' beliefs, values and feelings, they are more likely to formulate positive relationships. They are also more likely to learn from the diverse experience and backgrounds of others and contribute positively to the formulation of a tolerant and inclusive society.

## 5. Social Skills

This domain focuses upon building and maintaining positive relationships and the ability to problem solve in an effective and solution focused way. The strategies for forming and maintaining relationships include those skills of conflict management and the ability to reduce negative feelings and distraction when in the learning context or situation. Students are encouraged to use and understand how their interactions with others can improve their learning experience.

# The Key to School Improvement

Developing individuals' skills within these 5 domains are also key to school improvement. Social and emotional skills are essential for all students and staff in the school context – and not simply for those identified or labelled as having social, emotional or behavioural difficulties. According to the DCSF guidance booklet:

'The evidence is overwhelming that well-designed programmes to promote social and emotional skills can result in gains that are absolutely central to the goals of all schools, including:

- better academic results for all pupils and schools;
- more effective learning – some well-known programmes have been shown to have demonstrable and measurable effects on attainments of all pupils in reading, non-verbal reasoning, problem solving, learning-to-learn skills and maths;
- higher motivation;
- better behaviour;
- higher school attendance;
- more responsible pupils, who are better citizens and more able to contribute to society;
- lower levels of stress and anxiety;
- higher morale, performance and retention of staff;
- a more positive school ethos.'
(DCSF (2007) p. 8-9)

The positive and key role that SEAL adopts in the area of learning cannot be over estimated. The development of social and emotional skills are essential pre-requisites for the learning process. These skills evidently underpin effective learning by helping children to:

- 'learn to manage their impulses, help them settle quickly, concentrate and not disrupt others.
- build warm relationships, which help them to care what others (e.g. staff and peers) think and to respond positively to them.
- manage strong and uncomfortable emotions such as anger and frustration, and become more resilient, which helps them rise to the challenge of the learning process and stick at it if things get tough.
- learn to feel good about themselves, which reduces the likelihood of disruptive behaviour and increases capacity for independent learning.
- manage anxiety and stress, including how to deal with tests and examinations.
- learn to empathise, for example, with other pupils' desire to learn, which helps them contribute to a positive learning environment.
- reflect on longer-term goals, which helps them see the point of learning, raise their aspirations and become more able to resist negative pressure from others.
- feel optimistic about themselves and their ability to learn, which improves their motivation to work hard and attend regularly.'
(DCSF (2007) p.9)

Such children also develop higher levels of self-esteem and confidence and tend to present as happier and engaged in more positive relationships. A further positive outcome of such developments is an improvement in behaviour and attendance in the school context. (Weare and Gray, 2003; Zins et al, 2004)

## Building on SEAL

Whilst it is clearly evident that the SEAL approach and curriculum is vital in terms of supporting the development of social and emotional skills and in maintaining overall well-being and academic achievement, it is also important to highlight the need to further build upon these approaches – particularly in our specialist context in which the children's needs are significantly greater than those of their mainstream peers.

The SEAL resources consequently also provide opportunities to reinforce whole class activities in small group resources which can also be used to target those children who are deemed to be less socially and emotionally secure. However, working in such a focused manner can raise some sensitive issues – particularly amongst parents. We know that development is continually affected by life events – many of which are outside of both the control of the children and their parents. Traumatic events such as loss, neglect and violence will impact upon the development of social and emotional skills. Bringing up children within diverse, pressurised, economically challenged times and environments clearly has an impact upon behaviour and development. Our focus, therefore, is to support the development of these essential skills within a nurturing and secure context in which the children have ongoing opportunities to develop strong bonds with significant adults who continually model the skills of emotional literacy themselves.

This scheme of work is not intended to provide an alternative to the SEAL curriculum/approach, but rather to build upon this whilst also ensuring that our children are provided with an intensive programme of support. The practical nature of the nurturing approach i.e. the use of games, role play and practical activities also makes it particularly appealing and pertinent to the younger age range. The sessions are predictable, secure and practical and follow a set routine in order to ensure security and opportunities for reinforcement.

## Aims of the approach

The aims of the approach are as follows:

- To enable students to develop the basic skills of communication e.g. appropriate looking, listening, conversation and turn taking skills.
- To enable students to develop a vocabulary for basic emotions and to identify and gain an understanding of these feelings that we all regularly experience.
- To enable students to define a friend and to be able to make and sustain friendships.
- To model genuine and appropriate social and emotional responses for students.
- To enable students to feel valued and nurtured.
- To improve students' self-concept.
- To promote self-respect and respect for others differences and values.
- To encourage students to be reflective and to monitor and evaluate the development of their own skills.
- To enable students to identify and distinguish between appropriate and inappropriate social behaviours in a range of contexts.
- To reinforce appropriate and safe 'play' skills in a range of contexts.

The extent to which these aims are met, will perhaps indicate the success or otherwise of the approach and its delivery.

## The Structure of the Programme

The student's programme is structured into 5 parts which are stored under the 5 SEAL headings as previously described. There are 10 sessions in section and these are as follows:

### 1 Self-awareness
Session 1 - About Me
Session 2 – Coping With Stress
Session 3 – Calming Down
Session 4 – Being Relaxed
Session 5 – Protective Shields
Session 6 – Highlighting Skills
Session 7 – Making People Happy
Session 8 - Belonging
Session 9 - Helping Others
Session 10 – Taking Responsibility

### 2 Managing feelings
Session 1 – Angry and Sad
Session 2 – Coping With Sadness
Session 3 – Feeling Scared
Session 4 – Worry Busters
Session 5 – Stress Busters

Session 6 – Feeling Jealous
Session 7 - Bullying
Session 8 – Feeling Excited
Session 9 - Beat Boredom
Session 10 – Different Dilemmas

### 3 Motivation
Session 1 – Top ten Aims
Session 2 – Mighty Motivators
Session 3 – Keeping Fit
Session 4 – Taking Exercise
Session 5 - Achieving
Session 6 – Being a Leader
Session 7 – Releasing Anger and Stress
Session 8 – Defining Motivation
Session 9 - A Challenge and a Goal
Session 10 – Going for Gold

### 4 Empathy
Session 1 – Caring and Sharing
Session 2 – Problem Solving
Session 3 – What is a Problem?
Session 4 – Positive statements
Session 5 – Move It!
Session 6 – I Know Something
Session 7 – Recognising Helpers
Session 8 – Sharing is Important
Session 9 - Understanding Others feelings
Session 10 – Friends Anger

### 5 Social skills
Session 1 – Self Reflection
Session 2 – Locus of Control
Session 3 – Helping Friends
Session 4 – Favourite Games
Session 5 – Share Your problem
Session 6 – Listen Up!
Session 7 – Use Your Eyes
Session 8 – Listening and Talking
Session 9 - Friendship Games
Session 10 – A Good Friend

## The Structure of the Sessions

Each of the 10 sessions within each of the 5 sections is structured in a similar way and notes are provided for the facilitator in order to aid delivery. The structure of the sessions is usually as follows:
- Introduction Game
- Bag Game
- Activity/Activities (Activity Sheets)
- Game
- Closing Compliments

The number of activities/activity sheets/games does vary from session to session. The facilitator's notes also ensure that appropriate resources can be gathered prior to the start of the session e.g. items for each of the bag games and photocopies of relevant activity sheets for each member of the group. It is anticipated that sessions will run for approximately 35 minutes but the approach is intended to be flexible and it is anticipated that facilitators will judge the time required for each part of the session according to the nature and needs of the target group. We also feel that it is important to be flexible regarding the interest levels and motivation of the students. For example, if an activity is perceived as highly motivating and enjoyable then we would suggest additional time might be allocated and when an activity is perceived as overly demanding for some individuals then the time be reduced. Overall, the level of differentiation and delivery will clearly be based upon the experience, skills and judgement of the facilitators themselves.

## Closing Compliments

Every session ends with closing compliments and aims to provide each of the students with positive feedback. It will be important for the facilitator to ensure that each student is given a compliment and this may include highlighting the following behaviour or responses:

- Listening well and attentively
- Taking turns/waiting for a turn
- Showing empathy or concern for others
- Being thoughtful
- Supporting someone who found responding or contributing difficult

- Working hard in activities during the session
- Building on others' ideas and not putting anyone down
- Overcoming any initial embarrassment or fear and trying to contribute
- Being honest and reflective about themselves
- Making a contribution
- Having a go and being positive in the session

It would also be helpful to reinforce these positives by encouraging students to identify one thing that each member of the group has done well in the session. This could take the form of a Golden Scroll for each student in the group. For this activity, the facilitator needs to obtain a large piece of paper, approximately one metre in length, and a large gold marker pen. The name of the pupil can be written at the top of the paper and the facilitator then can go around the circle asking each student to say something positive about the student whose scroll it is. They can choose an attribute or a specific skill or something that the student has done well in the session. Then with the appropriate ceremony, the scroll can be awarded to the named student in the group.

As time constraints may not allow for each student to be awarded a golden scroll in each session, the facilitator may wish to identify, or ask the whole group to nominate one or more students at the end of the session. It will be vital to keep a record of this activity so as to ensure that all members of the group have been awarded a golden scroll within each of the five modules.

## A Final Point

The nurturing approach that we have adopted and the development of the social and emotional skills programme within this context remains a work in progress. This is, in no sense, intended to provide a definitive programme but does, hopefully, present practitioners with a truly practical and comprehensive approach for developing these essential life skills. In conclusion, it remains essential to reinforce the fact that 'Nurture group practitioners have played an invaluable, if low key, part in the development of education over the past 40 years. They have demonstrated a commitment to high-quality education for every child that predates Every Child Matters, and they believe passionately that this is achievable when there is a balance between both qualitative and quantitative aspects of education, when the relational and affective matter as much as the measurable' (Boxall (2002) p.31).

This remains our challenge and our primary objective in order to ensure the well-being and inclusion of our most vulnerable young people and to continue to build school environment embedded within the tenets of social inclusion.

## References

Berler, E.S., Gross, A.M., & Drabman, R.S. (1982) Social skills training with children: proceed with caution *Journal of Applied Behaviour Analysis*, 15, 41-53

Bennathan, M., and Boxall, M. (2000) *Effective Intervention in Primary Schools: Nurture Groups* Fulton

Bennathan, M., and Rose, J. (2008) *All About Nurture Groups* London: Nurture Group Network

Boxall, M. (1998) *The Boxall Profile: Handbook for Teachers* AWCEBD

Boxall, M. (2002) *Nurture Groups in Schools: Principles and Practice* Sage/Paul Chapman

Bruce, T. (1997) *Early Childhood Education* Hodder and Stoughton

Cartledge, G., & Milburn, J.F. (eds) (1980) *Teaching Social Skills to Children* New York: Pergamon Press

Cooke, T.P., & Apolloni, T. (1976) Developing positive social-emotional behaviours: A study of training and generalization effects

Journal of Applied Behaviour Analysis 9, 65-78

Cooper, P., Smith, C., and Upton, G. (1994) *Emotional and Behavioural Difficulties: Theory to Practice* Routledge

DES (1990) *Starting with Quality: report of the Commission of Enquiry into the quality of educational experiences offered to three and four year olds* HMSO

DCSF (2007) *2020 Vision: Teaching and Learning Review Group* DCSF

DCSF (2007) *Secondary National Strategy for School Improvement Social and Emotional Aspects of Learning for Secondary Schools (SEAL) Guidance Booklet*

DCSF (2007d) *Social and emotional aspects of learning for secondary schools: staff development booklet* DCSF

DCSF (2007e) *Social and emotional aspects of learning for secondary schools: theme 1: a place to learn Y7* DCSF

DCSF (2007f) *Social and emotional aspects of learning for secondary schools: further reading booklet* DCSF

DCSF (2009) *Learning Behaviour: Lessons Learned* London: The Stationery Office

Dowling, M. (2000) *Young Children's Personal, Social and Emotional Development* Chapman

Dunn, J. (1994) Understanding Others and the Social World: Current issues in development research and their relation to pre-school experience and practice *Journal of Applied Developmental Psychology* 15, (578-583)

Eisenber, N., Fabes, R., Murphy, B., Karbon, M., & Smith, M. (1996) The relations of children's disposition empathy related responding to their emotional regulation and social functioning *Developmental Psychology* 32(2), (192-209)

Elias, M.J., & Clabby, J. (1992) *Building Social Problem Solving Skills: Guidelines from a school based programme.* Josey-Bass

Faber, A., and Mazlish, E. (1982) *How to Talk so Kids will Listen and Listen so Kids Will Talk* Avon

Goleman, D. (1995) *Emotional Intelligence: Why it can matter more than IQ* London: Bloomsbury

Greenberg, M.T., & Kusche, C.A. (1993) *Promoting Social and Emotional Development in Deaf Children The PATH programme* Seattle University of California Press

Hand, B (2002) The benefits of eating together (Internet )
Available at www.sparkpeople.com

Hops, H., & Greenwood, C.R. (1981) Social skills deficit in Marsh, E.J., & Terdal, L.G. (eds) *Behavioural assessment of childhood disorders* New York: Guildford Press

Hyson, M.C. (1994) *The Emotional Development of Young Children: Building an Emotion Centred Curriculum* Teachers College Press London

Jackson, F.N., Jackson, A.D., & Monroe, C. (1983) *Program Guide Getting Along With Others Teaching Social Effectiveness to Children* Illinois: Research Press

LaGreca, A.M. & Santogrossi, D.A. (1980) Social skills training with elementary school students: A behavioural group approach *Journal for Consulting and Clinical Psychology*, 48, 220-227

Le Mare, L.J., & Rubin, K.H. (1987) Perspective taking and peer interaction: a structural analysis *Child Development* 58, (p 306-315)

Rae, T. (1998) *Dealing with Feeling An emotional literacy curriculum* Lucky Duck Publishing

Rinaldi, W. (1992) *The Social Use of Language Programme* NFER Nelson

Schroeder, A. (1996) *Socially Speaking* Cambs LDA

Rogers, B. (2000) *Classroom Behaviour* Books Education

Van Hasselt, V.B., Hersen, M., Whitehall, M.B., & Bellack, A.S. (1979) Social skill assessment and training for children An Evaluative Review Behaviour *Research and Therapy*, 17, 413-437

Weare, K. and Gray, G. (2003) *What works in developing children's emotional and social competence and wellbeing?* DfES

Zins, J., Weissberg, R., Wang, M. and Walberg, H. (2004) *Building academic success on social and emotional learning* Columbia: Teachers College

# Introductory PowerPoint - Training session for staff

**Nurturing Social and Emotional Skills**
**A programme to nurture development from**
**lower KS2 to lower KS3**
**A programme of work based upon nurturing principles**

**Aims of session**
- To provide participants with the rationale for developing the programme and adopting a 'nurturing' approach
- To highlight the importance and value of social skills training
- To outline the underlying philosophy and principles of nurture groups
- To present the physical set up of the nurture base and practicalities of employing nurturing principles in the whole school context
- To outline assessment and evaluation processes
- To describe the social and emotional skills programme and its arrangement under the five SEAL domains
- To provide an opportunity for participants to trial some of the resources/activities from the programme

---

**Context in which programme developed**

- A SEBD school
- Focus on relationships
- Extra-curricular activities
- Profile of students – insecure attachment
- Need for therapeutic interventions and access to nurturing principles within a nurture book

## The need for social skills training

- Social skills vital for development
- Turn taking, sharing, resolving conflicts, coping with anger, responding assertively and gaining confidence
- Skills need to be learnt in early years or 'gaps' in social, emotional and cognitive learning will occur (insecure attachment → 'gaps')
- Research supports the appropriate delivery of social skills interventions

## Nurture groups

- Inner London – 1969 – Marjory Boxall (EP)
- Link between social, emotional and behavioural difficulties and impoverished early nurturing
- Insecurely attached children's behaviour appropriate for children of younger chronological age
- Boxall (2002) – focus of nurture groups should be on building early attachments and the recreation of positive early care of child interactions

## Main nurturing principles – underpin the nurture group approach:

- Learning needs to be understood and responded to developmentally
- Classrooms offer safe and predictable environments with reliable adults who set firm boundaries
- Nurture promotes self-esteem
- Language is a key tool for communication – not simply a skill to be learnt
- All behaviour is a means of communication
- Transition is important in children's lives

## What is a nurture group?

- Inclusive early intervention to prevent development of social, emotional and behavioural difficulties
- Structured routines with homelike environment
- Offer model of relationships
- Staffed by two adults
- Short to medium term placements
- Maintain links with class
- Individualised support

## Layout and timetable for the nurture base

- 'Home' base – sofas/comfortable chairs, kitchen area, quiet area, cooking area, role play area and dining area
- Timetable – 'set' activities including toast time, games, introductions and set tasks and story time
- Behaviour 'modelled' by adults throughout the session

## Pre and post measures of children's development

- Need for systematic assessment
- Use of Boxall profile
- Development of pre and post intervention checklist for this social and emotional skills programme
- Measuring development in
  a) social behaviours
  b) management of feelings
  c) friendship skills
  d) social skills
- Need for regular updating

## Supporting SEAL – an important task

- SEAL – comprehensive approach to promoting social and emotional skills
- Use of whole school approach
- Direct and focussed learning opportunities
- Use of 'learning' to consolidate and teach skills
- CPD for whole staff
- Focus on sustaining and developing positive relationships

## Daniel Goleman's 5 Domains (1995)

- Self-awareness
- Managing feelings
- Motivation
- Empathy
- Social skills

The programme has been developed to build upon the SEAL approach whilst adopting nurturing principles and delivered within a nurturing context

### Key to school improvement

- Better academic results
- More effective learning
- Higher motivation
- Better behaviour
- Improved attendance
- Pupils as 'citizens'
- Reduction in stress and anxiety
- Higher morale, performance and retention of staff
- Positive school ethos

### Social and emotional skills programme

- 5 parts under 5 SEAL headings
- 10 sessions in each part
- Clear and consistent routine and structure
- 'Short' 30 minute sessions
- Practical approach which can be used flexibly

## Try it out!

- Introduction – Section 1 Session 2
- The Bag Game
- Getting Stressed Out – activity page
- The Fish Game
- Closing compliments

## Overall aims of the approach

- Developing communication skills
- Increasing vocabulary for emotions
- Developing friendship skills
- Modelling 'genuine' responses
- Increase level of nurturing
- Improve self-concept
- Promote respect
- Increase ability to reflect
- Distinguish between appropriate and inappropriate behaviours
- To increase 'safety' – emotional and physical (in and out of classroom context)

**A final reminder: nurture groups work!**

- Emotional well-being underpins learning
- Jim Rose (2007) – at least 1000 in primary and over 100 in secondary
- Glasgow evaluation (2007) – significant impact upon attendance, behaviour and academic achievement
- Vital in terms of ensuring the well-being of our most vulnerable children and young people

# Part 2 - The Programme

- **Section 1 Self-awareness**

- **Section 2 Managing Feelings**

- **Section 3 Motivation**

- **Section 4 Empathy**

- **Section 5 Social Skills**

# Section 1

## Self-awareness

# Section 1: Self-awareness

## Session 1
## Introduction – About Me! (5mins)

The facilitator can introduce themselves to the group by role modelling a 'personal introduction': I am Mr Henry. I am thirty two years of age and I like watching TV and playing football'. The students can be seated in a circle and in turn can then be encouraged to proceed with this activity, introducing themselves and providing three 'personal' facts about themselves to the group.

In this initial session, the facilitator can then provide a brief summary of the programme. It may be helpful to develop a short script for this purpose in order to highlight the following:

- This is a course especially designed for young people.
- We will be learning about ourselves and how to manage how we feel and act.
- We will also be learning about setting goals for ourselves and how we can stay motivated.
- Many of the activities will be good fun and enable us to learn how to take turns, to show respect for others' feelings and ideas and to become good friends.
- We will all be able to improve our social skills and the way we manage our feelings. This will help us to have good friendships and learn better in class.

## Group Rules (5 mins)

At the outset, it will be important for the facilitator to clarify group rules. This can be done by asking all the students in the group what they think the rules should be. They need to think about how they should behave in order to make sure that the group remains a comfortable place to be and a place in which they can engage in learning and developing their social, emotional and behavioural skills. It may be useful for the facilitator to record the students' ideas on a whiteboard or flipchart as appropriate and to prompt thinking by providing some initial ideas. These could be as follows:

- We listen to each other
- We wait our turn
- We try to build on each others' ideas
- We help each other to make contributions
- We share and take care of each other etc

## The Bag Game (5 mins)

The facilitator can next introduce the bag game. In this activity, a bag is passed around the circle containing a selection of pictures of famous people. The students are asked to take one picture and then, in turn, describe the famous person. They can be encouraged to use descriptive language, identifying colour and type of eyes, hair and clothes etc. It may be helpful for the facilitator to make use of a series of prompt questions as follows:

- Who is this?
- What do they do?
- Would you like to be like this person? If so, why? If not, why not?
- Do you think this person is proud/happy to be who they are?

The idea here is to encourage the development of language, turn taking and self-awareness. It is particularly important for the students to consider the individual's positive qualities and to begin to identify/clarify for themselves why they might like to develop such qualities.

## Who do I want to be? (10 mins)

The students can then be presented with the activity sheet 'Who do I want to be?' They are encouraged to draw and/label as appropriate a portrait of themselves as they would like to be i.e. the notion of the 'ideal' self. They may wish to be a famous footballer, a film star, a teacher, a mother, a millionaire etc. They can then identify some of the qualities or skills they might need to reach such an objective. These can either be recorded on the activity sheet around their self-portraits or alternatively each student can discuss their ideas in turn around the circle.

## Future Focus – My Top Target

In order to reach our ideals we have to know who we are – identifying our strengths and areas for development and being honest in this process. This then enables us to identify personal targets The facilitator can talk through the 'My Top Target' process and ask the students to identify a target making use of the five-step process. They can be encouraged to discuss their ideas with a partner and these can either be recorded on individual activity sheets or fed back verbally, in turn around the circle. If the latter option is chosen, the facilitator may wish to use the format to record each of the group members 'three steps'.

### Always finish with Closing Compliments
### See Page 18

### Try to make some of your own relevant to whatever has happened during the session

# The nurture group network
### helping children and young people to succeed

---

**Domain 1: Self-awareness**

**Session 1**

## OUR GROUP RULES

We all agree to keep the following rules in our group:

- 
- 
- 
- 
- 

Signed: _____ Date: _____

---

**Domain 1: Self-awareness**

**Session 1**

## THE BAG GAME

**A selection of photographs of famous people**
e.g. David Beckham
The Prime Minister
Posh Spice
The Headteacher!
Simon Cowell etc

---

**Domain 1: Self-awareness**

**Session 1**

## WHO DO I WANT TO BE?
### My 'Ideal' Self!
### A Portrait

---

**Domain 1: Self-awareness**

**Session 1**

## MY TOP TARGETS

Set you own target by going through the five-stepped approach:

**Step 1:** What do I want to do well?

**Step 2:** Who can help me?

**Step 3:** How can I help myself?

**Step 4:** How will I know I've improved - What will be different?

**Step 5:** What are my three small steps

**These are my three steps:**

1)
2)
3)

---

Copyright of the Nurture Group Network 2011

# Section 1: Self-awareness
# Session 2
# Introduction (5 mins)

At the outset the facilitator can reinforce the group rules ensuring that all the students in the group are fully aware of these. It then may be useful for the facilitator to ask the students to articulate their top target set in the previous session and to also give some feedback to the group as to how well they think they have done during the intervening period of time.

## The Bag Game (5 mins)

A selection of soft toys is passed round in the bag with each student being asked to take one at a time. They are then required to describe the soft toy that they have in their hands, making use of as much language as possible. The facilitator can prompt individuals in this; making reference to texture, shape, size and how the toy feels.

## Getting Stressed Out (10 mins+)

The activity sheet provides prompts for the students to consider and requires them to identify ways that they can help themselves when they feel upset and stressed by certain situations. They are presented with a series of strategies that they might be able to use and required to colour in each of those that they think they might find useful. They are also asked to identify some strategies of their own. They are finally required to identify their best 'stress buster' and why they have made this choice.

## The Fish Game (5 mins)

The facilitator can move the chairs so that the circle is horseshoe shaped. This will allow the students to move outside of the circle. The facilitator can next allocate each pupil a different fish name, for example, cod, hake, squid, octopus, halibut. The students are then given instructions by the facilitator. For example, on hearing the command "the tide's out squid", the squid have to rush out of the circle and run around clockwise and then back in through the gaps to a different chair. When they are halfway around the facilitator may say "tide's turning" and then the pupils will have to reverse direction. Alternatively, the facilitator may shout "tidal wave coming" and then students can go in either direction back into the circle which is intended to be the harbour. It may be possible at times to have sets of fish running simultaneously. The idea here is not only to promote listening skills but also to have fun and to set a positive tone for the session as a whole.

## Always finish with Closing Compliments (5 mins)
## See Page 18

## Try to make some of your own relevant to whatever has happened during the session

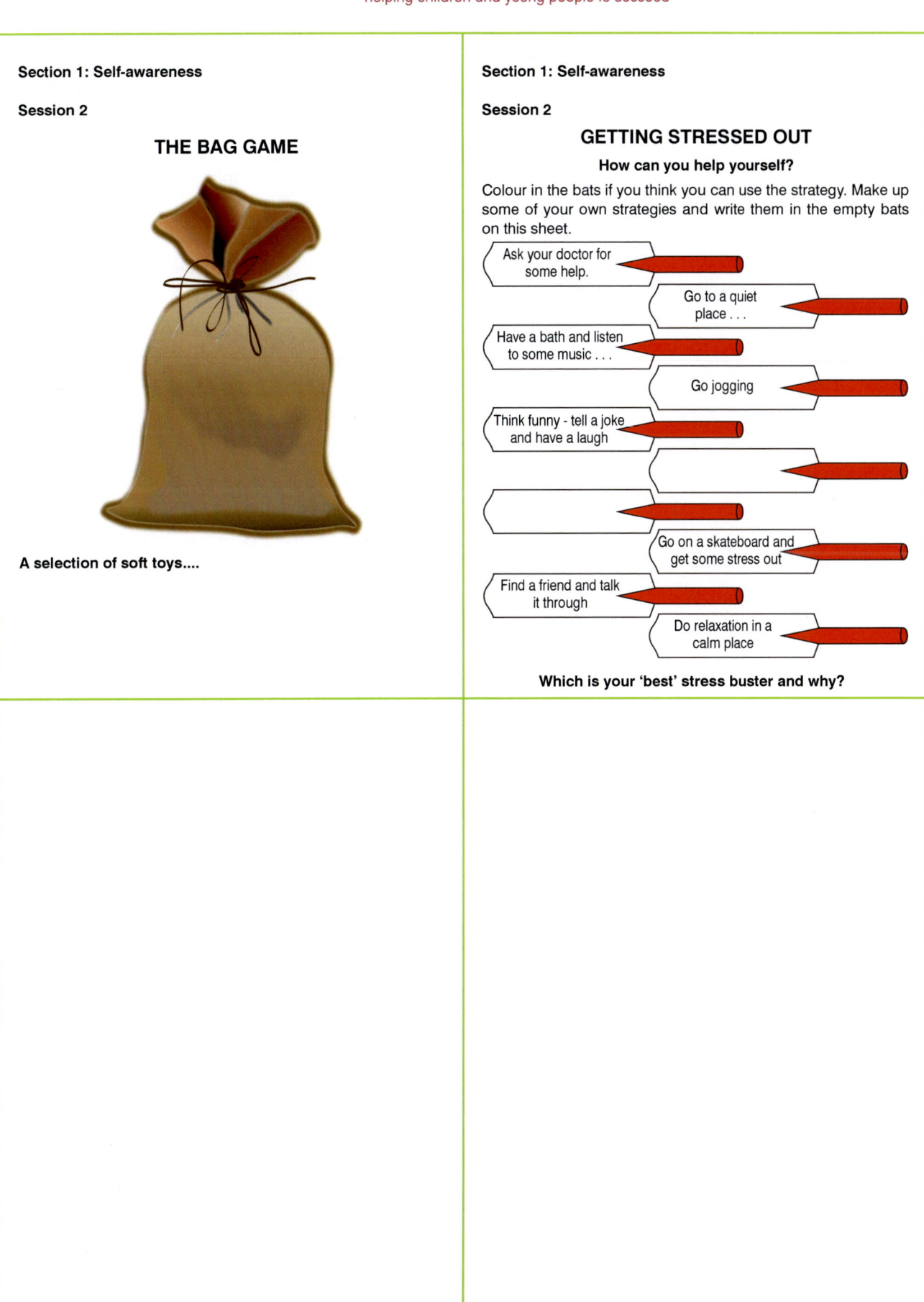

**Section 1: Self-awareness**

**Session 2**

## THE BAG GAME

**A selection of soft toys....**

---

**Section 1: Self-awareness**

**Session 2**

## GETTING STRESSED OUT

**How can you help yourself?**

Colour in the bats if you think you can use the strategy. Make up some of your own strategies and write them in the empty bats on this sheet.

- Ask your doctor for some help.
- Go to a quiet place . . .
- Have a bath and listen to some music . . .
- Go jogging
- Think funny - tell a joke and have a laugh
- Go on a skateboard and get some stress out
- Find a friend and talk it through
- Do relaxation in a calm place

**Which is your 'best' stress buster and why?**

# Section 1: Self Awareness
# Session 3
# Introduction

At the outset the Group rules can be reinforced with all members of the group. It may be useful to have these written up on a whiteboard and students can also have made their own posters which they can make reference to. The topic of this domain is being self aware of your feelings. The facilitator can encourage the students to discuss whether they have used any of the strategies introduced in the last session and if they have found any of these strategies useful. Have a discussion about anger and how it can explode (like a bomb), and also ask the students if they can visualise their own anger as a bomb. Then they can discuss whether they can think of strategies to try and control their anger more effectively, making reference to appropriately related activities from previous sessions.

## The Bag Game

The bag is passed around the group containing a set of situation pictures. These can include someone shouting at someone, someone giving someone a present, someone standing alone in a corner etc. The students are asked to pick one situation from the bag and explain how that situation would make them feel and if it would 'set off' their anger. It may be useful for the facilitator to ascertain as to whether or not all the students in the group agree with each student's individual triggers-how are they similar and how are they different?

## Bomb

In this activity the facilitator can reinforce the fact that there are times when we all feel angry. Remind the students that they are visualising their anger as a bomb and discuss what situations 'set off' their anger, write their ideas on the board so they are there to help them with the work. Then discuss as a group what would 'extinguish their fuse' i.e. calm them down.

The facilitator can encourage the students to take time to reflect on all ideas given forward and discuss which would work for them and which wouldn't and why.

## Bomb Worksheet

The facilitator can present the worksheet to the group, leaving the previous ideas on the board to support the students. The students can identify 3 things that they could do to avoid an explosion i.e. things that help them to calm down. They can then identify some strategies they could use to help a friend who may be about to explode, drawing pictures of these and labelling them.

**Always finish with Closing Compliments (5 mins)**
**See Page 18**
**Try to make some of your own relevant to whatever has happened during the session**

**Session 3:**

## THE BAG GAME

**Set of 'different situation' pictures ie:**
A child isolated
A child being shouted at
A child being given a present
Someone listening to someone else
Someone playing a game with someone else
A child being bullied

**Section 1: Self-awareness**

**Session 3**

## BOMB

What 3 things can I do to avoid the explosion?

1. _____
2. _____
3. _____

How can I help my friends? (Draw or label your ideas)

# Section 1: Self-awareness
# Session 4
# Introduction

At the outset the Group rules can be reinforced with all members of the group. The facilitator can introduce the session by discussing the contents of the previous session which anger was visualised as a bomb. The facilitator needs to focus on the latter part of the session of extinguishing the fuse. Ask the students how they calm down, and then ask them who likes time alone to help them calm down and manage their feelings. Discuss with the students whether they think clearly while they are upset. The facilitator can highlight the fact that it easier to solve problems when you are calm and when you can give yourself time to think.

## The Bag Game (5 mins)

The facilitator can next introduce the bag game. In this activity, a bag is passed around the circle containing a selection of pictures of calming activities that can help people to relax. The bag will be passed around the group and each student in turn will pick out a picture and discuss it as follows:
- Would this activity calm you?
- Would you find it relaxing?
- Do you think it would help you to calm down?
- Can you see why people find it relaxing?

The idea here is to encourage the development of language, turn taking and self-awareness. It is particularly important for the students to consider the individual's positive qualities and to begin to identify/clarify for themselves why they might like to develop such qualities.

## Me Time

The students can discuss how our bodies feel when we are relaxed. The facilitator can ask the students to name and describe a time when they feel really relaxed. Ask the students (as a group) to come up with strategies on how/where they can relax if there are people around. Write the ideas on the board as they are presented and identified.
Me Time – Activity Sheet

Look at the worksheet together discuss positive comments and drawings. It may be helpful to print off some pictures of relaxing activities or people relaxing for the less confident/literate students to stick onto the worksheet. The students will then complete the activity sheet and the facilitator can leave the ideas on the board in order to help them to label their work.

## Always finish with Closing Compliments (5 mins)
## See Page 18
## Try to make some of your own relevant to whatever has happened during the session

Section 1:

Session 4

**THE BAG GAME**

**Set of 'relaxation' pictures ie:**
Reading a book
Watching television
Sleeping
Playing games
Having a cup of tea

Section 1: Self-awareness

Session 4

**ME TIME**

Draw and label things that you can do to relax

# Section 1: Self-awareness
# Session 5
# Introduction

At the outset the Group rules can be reinforced with all members of the group. The facilitator can introduce the session and ensure that everybody feels confident and happy regarding the previous sessions and address any issues that may arise. The facilitator can explain that the topic of this session will be about protection guards. The facilitator can explain what a protection guard is and how it could support students in protecting themselves from anger and hurt.

## The Bag Game

The facilitator can then introduce the bag game. In this activity, a bag is passed around the circle containing a selection positive comments that could be meant for anyone. The students can all take a piece of paper from the bag and in turn discuss how it would make them feel if somebody made this comment to them.

The idea here is to encourage the development of language, turn taking and self-awareness. It is particularly important for the students to consider the individual's positive qualities and to begin to identify/clarify for themselves why they might like to develop such qualities.

## How Can I Create a Protective Shield?

The facilitator can then lead a discussion on what a protection guard such as a protective shield might do and how these might be used in everyday life. Students can discuss what makes them feel good about themselves? Can they think of a time when something happened that made them feel good? Or identify a comment someone made about them that made them feel good? The facilitator can write the students ideas on the board as they come up with them.

## My Protective Shield

The facilitator can look at the worksheet together with the students and discuss positive comments and drawings. The students can then complete the worksheet, and the facilitator can leave the ideas on the board in order to help the students to label their work.

**Always finish with Closing Compliments (5 mins)
See Page 18
Try to make some of your own relevant to whatever has happened during the session**

**Section 1: Self-awareness**

**Session 5**

## THE BAG GAME

**A selection of Positive comments, e.g:**
Good listener
Very tidy
Always smiling
Always happy

**Section 1: Self-awareness**

**Session 5**

## MY PROTECTION GUARD

Design your protection guard label and draw positive feelings that can protect you from angry ones.

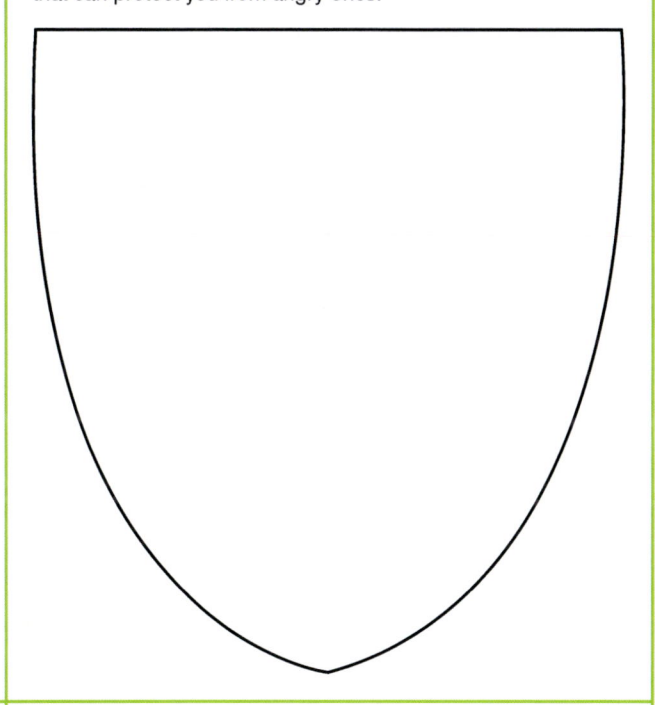

# Section 1: Self-awareness
# Session 6
# Introduction

At the outset the Group rules can be reinforced with all members of the group. The facilitator can introduce the session and ensure that all students feel confident and happy about the previous sessions and address any issues that may have arisen. The facilitator can then explain that the topic of today's session will be 'skills'. The facilitator can explain that a skill is something that you are good at and can be anything at all, academic, social, sporting, artistic etc.

## The Bag Game

The facilitator can next introduce the bag game. In this activity, a bag is passed around the circle containing a selection of everyday objects. Each student will pick an object from the bag and describe what skill you may need in order to use this object. For example if they pick out a pencil, the skill could be writing or drawing. The facilitator will encourage a discussion of other skills that students may exhibit in order to successfully use each of the objects.

The idea here is to encourage the development of language, turn taking and self-awareness.

## What are my skills?

The facilitator can then ask the students to sit down in the chairs which will have been arranged in a circle. They can then describe 1 thing that they have improved on during the last week. Each student can be provided with a copy of the certificate sheet to write on the achievement of another student from the group and the facilitator can prompt and propose if needed. The group can then be asked to identify what they are good at in school, and the facilitator can elicit a response from each student. Students can next identify what they are good at in the home, recording the ideas and contributions on A3 paper or the board.

Students can then return to the circle of chairs and the facilitator can ask them to sit down and get into pairs. The facilitator can then give out a role play card to each pair. Each pair can act out the skill described on the role-play card. The remainder of the group can then attempt to guess the skill being dramatised. They may ask 4 questions in this process but the answers must be only yes and no.

Each student can then be provided with a copy of the trophy activity sheet on which they can draw their best skill (that they are good at) and complete the sentence starter 'My best skill is . . . .'

## End Game

The facilitator can gather all the students then on the chairs (circled) and tell them that they are all going to stand and must then sit down one by one with no talking until everyone is seated. (They cannot discuss who goes when or in which order and if anyone moves at the same time then they all have to stand again.

**Always finish with Closing Compliments (5 mins)**
**See Page 18 Try to make some of your own relevant to whatever has happened during the session**

Section 1: Self-awareness

Session 6

## THE BAG GAME

**A selection of everyday objects that require a skill, e.g**

Pencil
Paint Brush
Book
Plastic knife and fork
Gardening implements

---

Section 1: Self-awareness

Session 6

## ROLE PLAY CARDS

- I am good at tidying up
- I am good at looking after things
- I am good at taking care of others
- I am good at sports
- I am good at listening to adults
- I am good at sharing
- I am good at writing neatly
- I am good at behaving sensibly

---

Section 1: Self-awareness

Session 6

## CERTIFICATE ACTIVITY SHEET

I think you are good at

---

Session 1: Self-awareness

Session 6

MY BEST SKILL IS

---

Copyright of the Nurture Group Network 2011

47

# Section 1: Self-awareness
# Session 7
# Introduction

At the outset the Group rules can be reinforced with all members of the group. The facilitator can introduce the session and ensure that everybody feels confident and happy about the previous session and address any issues that may have arisen. The facilitator can then explain that the topic of this session will be on understanding your behaviour and what impact our behaviour may have on others.

## The Bag Game

The facilitator can then introduce the bag game. In this activity, a bag is passed around the circle containing a selection of bad reactions people have/display when they are angry. The students will all pick one of these reactions cards out of the bag and in turn describe the situation and discuss how it would make them feel if someone reacted like that to others in their group.

The idea here is to encourage the development of language, turn taking and self-awareness. It is particularly important for the students to consider the individual's positive qualities in terms of managing such strong and uncomfortable feelings and to begin to identify/clarify for themselves why they might like to develop such qualities.

## Understanding

The facilitator can discuss with the group if there has been a time when they have made someone else happy – how did they know that person was happy? Then students can discuss when they have made someone else feel angry. The facilitator can write notes and ideas on the board in order to support the students in completing the subsequent activity sheet.
Finally the facilitator can pose the following question to the group: Are there things that you do often that make people angry/happy ?

## Understanding – Activity Sheet

The facilitator can next present the activity sheet to the group and discuss positive comments and drawings.

The students can be encouraged to complete the activity sheet, with support where needed, with the facilitator recording their ideas and contributions on the board in order to help the students to label their work.

## Always finish with Closing Compliments (5 mins)
## See Page 18
## Try to make some of your own relevant to whatever has happened during the session

**Section 1: Self-awareness**

**Session 7**

## THE BAG GAME

**A selection of pictures of bad reactions to anger, e.g.**

Throwing things
Hitting things
Crying
Shouting at someone

---

**Section 1: Self-awareness**

**Session 7**

**Activity Sheet**

## UNDERSTANDING EACH OTHER

Write or draw in the boxes

| Others get angry when ... | Others make me angry when ... |

| What can I do to not make them angry? | What can they do to help me? |

---

Copyright of the Nurture Group Network 2011

# Section 1: Self-awareness
# Session 8
# Introduction

At the outset the Group rules can be reinforced with all members of the group. The facilitator can introduce the session and ensure that everybody feels confident and happy regarding the content and outcomes of the previous session and also address any issues that may have arisen. The facilitator can explain that the topic of today's session will be belonging and how it feels to be a part of a group or community.

## The Bag Game

The facilitator can then introduce the bag game. In this activity, a bag is passed around the circle containing a selection of pictures of different buildings or groups. The students will each pick an item to initially describe to the group. They will then need to identify whether this is a group that they would like to belong to and articulate their reasons for making such a judgement.

The idea here is to encourage the development of language, turn taking and self-awareness. It is particularly important for the students to be able to make use of language to support their judgements and choices and the facilitator may wish to model some responses e.g. I would like to belong to Scouts because I think they do fun things and they also help people in the community.

## Belonging

The facilitator can then discuss with the group whether or not they see the school as a community and if they feel happy and safe within it. What one thing would they take with them from this school to an 'ideal' school? The facilitator can reinforce the importance of honest discussion, collecting student's idea. They can then discuss what they would leave behind, explaining their feelings and reasons for their selections.

## Belonging – Petal

The facilitator can then provide each student with the 'petals' activity sheet on which they can write/draw ideas. The students will be writing or drawing what they feel makes them feel happy and safe on the petals. The facilitator can then produce a large plant drawn onto card which will be ready for display and then ask the students to stick their petals on the top of the plant in order to form a flower.

**Always finish with Closing Compliments (5 mins)**
**See Page 18**
**Try to make some of your own relevant to whatever has happened during the session**

Section 1: Self-awareness

Session 8

**THE BAG GAME**

**A selection of different buildings or groups, e.g.**

School
Church
Football Team
Sports Hall
Scouts

Section 1: Self-awareness

Session 8

**BELONGING**

Write or draw in the petal what makes you feel happy or safe to be part of a group.

Copyright of the Nurture Group Network 2011

# Section 1: Self-awareness
# Session 9
# Introduction

The facilitator can introduce the session and ensuring that everybody feels confident and happy regarding the previous session and address any issues that may have arisen in the meantime. The facilitator can then explain that the topic of today's session will be that of helping others. The facilitator can then pose the following questions: What can the students do to help others? Who can the students help and why might it be important to do this?

## The Bag Game

The facilitator can then introduce the bag game. In this activity, a bag is passed around the circle containing a selection of pictures of different things that people can do to help others. For example, washing up, tidying their room, listening, sharing etc. The students can pick a picture from the bag and discuss how this activity/act helps others and who they know they could do this for both in and out of the school context.

The idea here is to encourage the development of language, turn taking and self-awareness. It is particularly important for the students to consider the individual's positive qualities in behaving in such helpful ways and to begin to identify/clarify for themselves why they might like to develop such qualities themselves.

## Helping Others

The facilitator can next arrange the chairs into a circle and start the discussion, by asking and answering the following question: what can I do to help others? The students can discuss this for a little while and then the facilitator can ask each student to finish the sentence, 'At school a job I do to help others is .... '. The facilitator must make sure that they allow the students time to think. When this circle round is completed the facilitator can change the sentence to, 'I help . . . . . . . . . . . . . . when I do this job'.

## I Do Help Others

When the group circle discussion has been completed the facilitator can next ask the students to have think about what they do out of school in order to help others. The students can then complete the activity sheet, writing and drawing things that they can do to help others.
When the activity sheets are completed the facilitator can arrange the chairs into a circle again and then gather the students back. The facilitator can pose the following questions: does it make you feel good to help others and why? How do you think the person that you are helping feels?

**Always finish with Closing Compliments (5 mins)**
**See Page 18**
**Try to make some of your own relevant to whatever has happened during the session**

**Section 1: Self-awareness**

**Session 9**

# THE BAG GAME

**A selection of pictures of things that help others, e.g.**

Washing up
Tidying room
Listening

**Section 1: Self-awareness**

**Session 9**

# I CAN HELP OTHERS

Write or draw and label things you can do to help others.

# Section 1: Self-awareness
# Session 10
# Introduction

At the outset the Group rules can be reinforced with all members of the group. The facilitator can introduce the session and ensure that everybody feels confident and happy about the previous session and address any issues that may have arisen. The facilitator can then explain that this session is intended to be a follow on from session 9 and that the group will be asked to talk about who does the jobs they could do. The facilitator can pose the question, 'What are the jobs that could you do that would make you a more responsible person?' The facilitator can elicit the students responses and record these on the board for further reference and prompting in this session.

## The Bag Game

The facilitator can next introduce the bag game. In this activity, a bag is passed around the circle containing a selection of different things that can be used to help others e.g. a toothbrush, a duster, an ear (plastic!), a bin bag etc. The students can then pick an item from the bag and discuss what they think the job could be that relates to the item, who they know who does the job now and if they think they themselves could take on the responsibility entailed in this job – either now or in the future .

The idea here is to encourage the development of language, turn taking and self-awareness. It is particularly important for the students to consider the individual's positive qualities in terms of helping others and to begin to identify/clarify for themselves why they might like to develop such qualities.

## Taking Responsibility

The facilitator can then arrange the chairs into a circle and ask each student in turn to take some time to look at the picture chart. They can then discuss as a group the jobs from the chart that they could do that would make them more responsible. The students can then complete the differentiated activity sheets. The confident writers in the group can complete the writing sheet provided, whilst the less able students can cut out the pictures of jobs from the sheet that they think they could do and then stick them on the grid provided.

## I Will Take Responsibility

The facilitator can next regroup the students to the circled chairs and finish with a discussion about what individual students will do to take more responsibility and describe how doing this will make them feel.

**Always finish with Closing Compliments (5 mins)
See Page 18
Try to make some of your own relevant to whatever has happened during the session**

## Section 1: Self-awareness

Session 10

### THE BAG GAME

**A selection of items that help you do jobs e.g.**

A duster
A bin bag
An ear

## Section 1: Self-awareness

Session 10

### TAKING RESPONSIBILITY

Here is a chart with some pictures of jobs that you can do to be more responsible. Can you make your own chart? You can use some of these picutres and make some of your own too.

## Section 1: Self-awareness

Session 10

### TAKING RESPONSIBILITY

I can become more responsible by doing more jobs.
Here are some jobs that I can do.

## Section 1: Self-awareness

Session 10

### TAKING RESPONSIBILITY

I will _____

I will _____

I will _____

I will _____

Copyright of the Nurture Group Network 2011

# Section 2

# Managing feelings

# Section 2: Managing Feelings
# Session 1
# Introduction

The facilitator can once again reinforce the group rules. It may be useful to have these written up on a whiteboard and students can also have made their own posters which they can make reference to. The topic of this domain is the management of feelings. The facilitator may wish to introduce this by engaging in a 'guess my feeling' game. He/she can make a variety of different faces and ask the students to guess how they are feeling by observing both their face and body language.

## The Bag Game

The bag is passed around the group containing a set of feelings faces pictures. These can include the feelings of happiness, excitement, fear, jealousy etc. The students are asked to pick one face and then to describe what this face would represent to them. It may be useful for the facilitator to ascertain as to whether or not all the students in the group agree with each student's individual assessment.

## Angry and Sad

In this activity the facilitator can reinforce the fact that there are times when we all feel angry and sad. We can sometimes experience these uncomfortable feelings simultaneously and it can be quite distressing at times. However there are ways in which we can help ourselves. The students can be introduced to a range of strategies including:

- Think funny
- Burn it up
- Use post-it notes
- Use traffic lights
- Listen up
- Count it down
- Talk it out

The facilitator can describe each of these in detail and then go around the circle asking students which ones they think they might use. They can also reflect upon a time when they may have used such a strategy in the past and if they didn't use such a strategy what might have happened had they had access to this information at the time and been able to more successfully cope with this situation.

## Fish and Chips Game

The facilitator will need to have prepared this activity in advance. A series of cars or pictures should be collected. The facilitator writes on the top and bottom of each card half a name of a well-known meal, e.g. on the top half of the card can be written 'fish' and on the bottom half o the card 'chips'. The card can then be cut into two. Other examples may include scrambled/egg, pork/pie, ice/cream or cheese/burger. There should be enough of these cards for the pupils to have one half each. The cards are shuffled initially and then one half of the card given to each pupil in the circle. The aim of the game is for the pupils to move around the circle in silence in order to find the other half of the card. As soon as each pair has found each other they are required to sit down next to each other.

### Always finish with Closing Compliments (5 mins)
### See Page 18
### Try to make some of your own relevant to whatever has happened during the session

**Section 2: Managing Feelings**

**Session 1**

## THE BAG GAME

**A set of 'feelings faces' pictures**
Happy
Sad
Angry
Bullied
Excited
Frightened
Jealous
Friendly

---

**Section 2: Managing Feelings**

**Session 1**

## ANGRY AND SAD

Sometimes we can feel angry and sad at the same time and it can be very uncomfortable. We can try to help ourselves in different ways. Tick the strategies you might use.

| THINK FUNNY | BURN IT UP! |
|---|---|
| Think of something funny or something that made me feel happy before. | Go and do some exercise to burn away the unhappiness. |

| USE TRAFFIC LIGHTS! | USE POST-IT NOTES! |
|---|---|
| Tell myself to stop and think so I can make a plan for myself. | Write down why I'm sad and angry and then work our my plan. |

| LISTEN UP! | COUNT IT DOWN! |
|---|---|
| Listen to calm, gentle music in a quiet place. | Count to 10, 20, 100 and take deep breaths - letting them out slowly. |

Talk to a friend about it. Think of a time when you felt sad and angry at the same time. Why was this? what did you do? How did things turn out? Would you do anything differently next time?

| TALK IT OUT! |
|---|
| Talk through the problem with someone I trust and like. |

# Section 2: Managing Feelings
# Session 2
# Introduction

The facilitator can reinforce the group rules and then engage the students in a circle round asking the question 'What makes people feel sad?' It is important that the students are not asked initially what makes them feel sad. The idea here is to reinforce the fact that every human being experiences this emotion at some point in their lives and there are many reasons as to why this would be the case.

## The Bag Game

The bag is handed around the circle containing a selection of clothes such as a sock, a t-shirt, a glove etc. The students are then asked to describe each of these items in turn imagining that they are doing this to an alien from outer space who does not understand English. The idea here is to encourage the use of vocabulary.

## Sad Sid

In this activity the students are presented with a scenario which describes how Sidney is feeling very sad because his best friend has left school. He is also isolated from his peers because he has one leg shorter than the other and is unable to play football. The students are asked how they would feel if they were in Sid's shoes and also identify ways in which they could help him: what is it that they would say and do? This activity can either be done by students working in smaller groups or with the facilitator taking the lead and recording their responses on a whiteboard or flipchart.

## Animal Antics

The students sitting around the circle are numbered 1, 2, 3, 4; 1, 2, 3, 4; etc. The facilitator then tells the group that No 1's are storks who cross the circle on one leg, the No 2's are humans who cross on two legs, the No 3's are monkeys who can cross on two legs and an arm and the No 4's are horses who cross on all fours. The facilitator then calls out numbers and the pupils are required to move across the circle and end up in different seats.

**Always finish with Closing Compliments (5 mins)**
**See Page 18**
**Try to make some of your own relevant to whatever has happened during the session**

Section 2: Managing Feelings

Session 2

## SAD SID

Sid feels very sad because his best friend has left school. He has moved up to Scotland. Sid misses him. He doesn't have any other friends because he doesn't play football because he has to wear a special shoe as one of his legs is shorter than the other. He can't run or kick a ball like the others boys. He feels lonely and sad but doesnt know what to do.

- How would you feel if you were in Sid's shoes?
- How could you help him?
- What would you say and do? (Use problem solving format)

---

Section 2: Managing Feelings

Session 2

## THE BAG GAME

**A selection of clothes:**

Sock
T-shirt
Glove etc

# Section 2: Managing Feelings
# Session 3
# Introduction

The facilitator can reinforce the group rules which can also be written up onto the white board. Once again, this session will focus upon feelings and times when we all feel frightened. It may be useful for the facilitator to introduce this feeling via a quick sentence completion round as follows: I felt frightened when - In order to take away any embarrassment or reluctance on the part of some students to admit to experiencing this feeling. Fear needs to be presented as having evolutionary significance in that it keeps us safe from danger.

## The Bag game

The bag is passed around the group containing a set of 'scary' animals. These can include a dinosaur, a grizzly bear, a lion, etc. The students are asked to pick one animal and to describe it in detail. What is it about this animal that makes them frightening to most human beings? It may be helpful for the facilitator to point out similarities and differences in the student's descriptions.

## When I feel scared

In this activity the facilitator can encourage the students to reflect upon the strategies that they may use in order to cope with situations that make them feel afraid. This will involve identifying self calming strategies alongside the people who may be able to help them in such situations. They can work through the following questions, recording their ideas on the format provided:
- When do I feel afraid?
- What can I do to help myself?
- What can others do to help me?

Ideas can be written or drawn as appropriate. The idea here is to highlight the fact that we all feel frightened at times and that there are ways in which we can help ourselves i.e. positive thinking, reframing, deep breathing, being assertive, asking a friend to support us, sharing our fear with a friend and engaging in joint problem solving.

## Pass the Feeling action game

The facilitator should arrange the students in a circle and model this game at the outset. This involves miming a feeling to the person sitting next to them in the circle and that person then having to mime the feeling with an action. For example, if the first person mimes feeling afraid, then the second person should mime cleaning their teeth when they are afraid and so on until the feeling has been passed and actioned around the whole circle.

## Always finish with Closing Compliments (5 mins)
## See Page 18
## Try to make some of your own relevant to whatever has happened during the session

**Section 2: Managing Feelings**

**Session 3**

## THE BAG GAME

**A selection of scary animals:**

Dinosaur
Lion
Snakes
Tiger
Crocodile
Shark etc

**Section 2: Managing Feelings**

**Session 3**

Think about times when you have felt afraid and complete your responses to the following 3 questions in the boxes below:

**I feel afraid when**

**What can I do to help myself?**

**What can others do to help me?**

# Section 2: Managing Feelings
# Session 4
# Introduction

When we feel anxious or worried we may often bottle these feelings up and make things worse for ourselves in the long run. Sometimes we can stop feeling worried and anxious quite quickly if we simply talk to a friend or teacher. The facilitator can introduce this session to the students by presenting them with a worry box. Each student can anonymously record a worry on a slip of paper which is then posted into the box. These can then be taken out and read aloud by the facilitator one at a time and the students can be asked to problem solve each of these worries in turn. What is it that the individual might do, say or think differently in order not to feel so worried. Once again, the notion of peer support and the importance of joint problem solving are emphasised.

## The Bag Game

The bag is passed around the group containing a series of pictures. These will all illustrate times when human beings might experience feelings of anxiety or worry and could typically include pictures of the following:
- Someone walking home alone on a dark night
- Someone begging for money
- Someone starting a new school
- Someone watching their parents fighting/arguing
- Someone going to the dentist
- Someone being bullied

The students can describe these situations in turn and then think about what each individual might need to do in order to cope more effectively. What strategies might they use? What has happened to make them feel this way and who might also help them to cope more effectively?

## Worry Busters

In this activity the students are asked to design posters on the format provided entitled Worry Busters. They can identify all the different ways in which people can or might cope with their feelings of worry and anxiety. For example:
- Talking it through
- Thinking positive
- Deep breathing
- Visualisation
- Writing it down
- Taking time out
- Using the traffic light method

## Musical faces game

The facilitator can have prepared a selection of music which reflects a range of different emotions and feelings. For example, Whiter Shade of Pale, She loves me, Somewhere over the rainbow etc. The students can be asked to formulate the appropriate face to match the feelings they feel are expressed in the music. It will be interesting for the facilitator to highlight any differences and similarities in responses. Do we all feel the same way about the same pieces of music or does music engender person specific responses?

**Always finish with Closing Compliments (5 mins)**
**See Page 18**
**Try to make some of your own relevant to whatever has happened during the session**

**Section 2: Managing Feelings**

**Session 4**

# THE BAG GAME

**A selection of pictures reflecting anxiety and worry for individuals including:**

- Someone walking home alone on a dark night
- Someone begging for money
- Someone starting a new school
- Someone watching their parents fighting/arguing
- Someone going to the dentist
- Someone being bullied

**Section 2: Managing Feelings**

**Session 4**

# WORRY BUSTERS POSTER

# Section 2: Managing Feelings
# Session 5
# Introduction

The facilitator can reinforce the group rules at the outset prior to introducing the feeling of stress to the group. Stress is experienced by all human beings at some point in their lives and is a particularly uncomfortable feeling when it gets out of control. However, many psychologists will tell us that we do need to experience some stress if we are to cope with challenge and develop our skills and abilities. It is when these feeling overwhelm us that we can have a problem and become sick – both mentally and physically. It is therefore important to be aware of the signs of stress and then try to reduce these feelings as soon as possible. The facilitator can ask the students to initially describe what happens to human when they get stressed? What are the physical and emotional symptoms? These can be recorded on a flip chart if appropriate.

## The Bag Game

The bag (large size) is passed around the group containing a range of sports equipment such as a tennis ball, a bat, a soft ball, a football, a cricket wicket, a shuttlecock, etc. The students are asked to pick one in turn and then describe it to the rest of the group making reference to size, shape and use. The facilitator can reinforce the fact that exercise is a very good stress buster.

## Stress Busters

In this activity the facilitator can ask the students to think of ways of managing or beating stress. What works for people? The students can share ideas and the facilitator may want to prompt them by providing a range of stress busters which may be helpful:

Taking exercise  
Relaxation scripts  
Talking it through  
Having time out  
Visualising a calm and peaceful place  
Using Traffic lights  
Counting it down  
Listen to music  

The students can then draw and label pictures in the frame provided entitled 'My calm and peaceful place'.

## Change Places Game

The facilitator can seat the students as for a circle time. In this game they can be asked to stand up and change places if they have had a happy experience, felt sad, beaten stress, felt excited, wanted to make someone else feel happy etc. The facilitator can try to ensure that all the students have a chance to move around by making reference to as many different feelings as possible.

## Always finish with Closing Compliments (5 mins)
## See Page 18
## Try to make some of your own relevant to whatever has happened during the session

**Section 2: Managing Feelings**

**Session 5**

## THE BAG GAME

A range of sports equipment such as a tennis ball, a bat, a soft ball, a football, a crickets wicket, a shuttlecock, etc.

**Section 2: Managing Feelings**

**Session 5**

## MY CALM AND PEACEFUL PLACE

# Section 2: Managing Feelings
# Session 6
# Introduction

The facilitator can reinforce the group rules prior to asking the students to consider and identify someone whom others may be jealous of. What is it about this person that would make others feel this way? The students can think of a range of famous people or celebrities that they admire such as David Beckham, Prince William, Adele, Lady GaGa, Ant and Dec, Simon Cowell, Cheryl Cole etc. They can identify factors such as appearance, wealth, visibility etc.

## The Bag Game

The bag is passed around the group containing photos of a range of celebrities as described above. The students are asked to pick one photo each and to then describe this person and the qualities that they have that make them famous. It may be helpful for the facilitator to highlight some of the similarities that these celebrities have such as wealth, talent, work ethic, social skills, passion etc.

## Jealous Jamie

In this activity the facilitator can read the problem page letter which is from Jamie who is feeling jealous because his best friend has decided to make friends with another boy who is new to the school. Jamie feels angry, jealous, hurt and upset. The students are asked to formulate a response to Jamie taking on the role of an Agony Aunt or Uncle. This can be written onto the format provided or fed back verbally to the Facilitator.

## Throw it game

The facilitator will need to provide a large soft ball and ensure that the students are standing in a circle, facing each other and all able to see each other. When the facilitator tells them to begin, one student who has the ball, can throw it to another student in the circle, shouting his/her name prior to throwing. The idea here is to promote concentration and attention whilst having some fun. Also, the students can be encouraged to do this as quickly as possible.

**Always finish with Closing Compliments (5 mins)**
**See Page 18**
**Try to make some of your own relevant to whatever has happened during the session**

**Section 2: Managing Feelings**

**Session 6**

## THE BAG GAME

**A range of photos of famous people or celebrities such as:**
David Beckham
Prince William
Adele
Lady GaGa
Ant and Dec
Simon Cowell
Cheryl Cole etc.

**Section 2: Managing Feelings**

**Session 6**

## JEALOUS JAMIE

Dear Dallas,
I hope you can help me. I am so fed up as my best friend Billy doesn't hang around with me anymore since he has become friends with the new boy Douglas. He says that Douglas is really great and a totally brilliant friend as they play football for the same junior team and his parents are really rich so they get treated to stuff all the time. I feel really jealous and so fed up because he doesn't want me around anymore. What can I do? I really hate feeling like this so please can you help me? What can I do?

### YOUR RESPONSE

# Section 2: Managing Feelings
# Session 7
# Introduction

The facilitator can reinforce group rules and present the topic for this session which is feeling bullied. This is clearly a sensitive issue and will need to be handled carefully, particularly if the facilitator is aware of any student having to contend with such behaviour at the current point in time.

Students can be asked to focus upon the following question; why do people bully others? The facilitator may wish to prompt initial responses by providing some ideas such as being jealous, feeling bad about themselves, feeling hurt or angry and wanting others to feel the same way too.

## The Bag Game

The bag is passed around the group containing a range of direction cards on which is printed a simple direction for the students to follow. For example, make a happy face, mime cleaning your teeth in an aggressive way, mime eating your lunch in a happy way, mime coming into the room in an excited way. As each student follows the directions on their card, the others have to try and guess the feeling.

## Bully Boy

In this activity the students are presented with a scenario in which Mickie, who is a new boy in the school is bullied by the rest of his class who all think that he is a little wimp who can't play football. He is getting very upset and doesn't want to come in as they took his mobile phone and hit him around the head the previous week. One boy in particular (Jamie) seems to be taking a lead in this and encouraging the others to bully Mickie. The students are asked to consider this problem and try to work out a plan of action for Mickie. What should he do first, second and third and who should he ask for help?

## Spin it game

The facilitator can place a bottle in the middle of a circle in which students are seated – preferably on the floor. The bottle can then be spun around until it stops. The student who is then directly facing the bottle can be asked a question by the facilitator as follows:

What makes you happy?
What makes you sad?
What makes you feel bullied?
What excites you?
What makes you feel loved? Etc.

**Always finish with Closing Compliments (5 mins)**
**See Page 18**
**Try to make some of your own relevant to whatever has happened during the session**

**Section 2: Managing Feelings**

**Session 7**

## THE BAG GAME

**A range of direction cards on which is printed a simple direction for the students to follow.**

Make a happy face
Mime cleaning your teeth in an aggressive way
Mime eating your lunch in a happy way
Mime coming into the room in an excited way

---

**Section 2: Managing Feelings**

**Session 7**

## BULLY BOY

Mickie is a new boy in the school and is being bullied by the rest of his class who all think that he is a little wimp who can't play football. He is getting very upset and doesn't want to come in as they took his mobile phone and hit him around the head last week. One boy in particular (Jamie) seems to be taking a lead in this and encouraging the others to bully Mickie.

Can you work out a plan of action for Mickie. What should he do first, second and third and who should he ask for help?

1.

2.

3.

People he should ask for help:

# Section 2: Managing Feelings
# Session 8
# Introduction

The facilitator can reinforce the group rules and present the topic for this session which is feeling excited. The students can be asked to thought-storm the following question: What makes us feel excited? It may be helpful to provide a few examples such as going to a party, having a surprise, going on a school trip, It will also be useful to focus upon the things that happen to our bodies when we experience this feeling such as a faster heart beat, quicker breathing, a flushed face etc.

## The Bag Game

The bag is passed around the group containing a range of situation cards which depict events and situations which might be exciting for the students. These can be in the form of picture cards and include pictures of the sea side, a fairground, a school play, a school trip, a farm yard, a variety of games and sporting events etc. The students can then describe these in turn and identify why these might be exciting things to do.

## Rank it!

In this activity the students are presented with a list of activities and are asked to rank these in order from 1-10 as to how exciting they would find them. The activities are presented on an illustrated list sheet with space for the students to record their ranking orders. Once this is completed, it may be interesting for the individuals to feedback to the whole group with the facilitator acting as scribe. This process should allow for the identification of similarities and differences and the most popular and exciting event for the group as a whole. Once again, this may also confirm the fact that we do not always share the same preferences and that any such differences need to be celebrated and respected.

## Afloat in a Boat Game

In this game the students are seated in a circle and provided with an object to pass round. As they pass the object around they say '(the number of students in the circle) were afloat in a boat, there was a loud shout and one fell out. The student who is holding the object when the word 'out' is shouted moves to sit in the circle. The game continues, reducing the number of children by 1 each time. However, the students who are out have the opportunity to get back in the boat by guessing the person who will be out next time. If they are correct, then they can swap places with that student. If more than 1 student guesses correctly then the Facilitator can make a decision as to who swaps places.

## Always finish with Closing Compliments (5 mins)
## See Page 18
## Try to make some of your own relevant to whatever has happened during the session

**Section 2: Managing Feelings**

**Session 8**

## THE BAG GAME

**A range of situation cards which depict events and situations which might be exciting for the students. These can be in the form of picture cards and include pictures of:**

Seaside
A Fairground
A School Play
A School Trip
A Farm Yard
A Variety of Games
A Sporting Event

---

**Section 2: Managing Feelings**

**Session 8**

## RANK IT!

Which is the most exciting for you? Rank order the 10 situations below:

1. Going to the seaside

2. Having a new game

3. Buying new clothes

4. Finding a new friend

5. Going to a party

6. Playing your favourite sport

7. Buying sweets

8. Going on an aeroplane

9. Winning a competition

10. Going on a school trip

# Section 2: Managing Feelings
# Session 9
# Introduction

The facilitator can reinforce the group rules and present the topic for this session which is feeling bored. The students can be asked to thought-storm the following question: What makes us feel bored? It may be helpful to provide a few examples such as work that we find hard, school holidays when we have no one to hang out with, teachers who do not make the lessons interesting, people who moan etc., It will also be useful to focus upon the things that happen to our bodies when we experience this feeling such as a experiencing lethargy, moving more slowly, day dreaming, fidgeting or inability to concentrate etc.

# The Bag Game

The bag is passed around the group containing a range of different coloured and shaped balloons e.g. red, green, yellow, gold, purple, long, round, oval, large small etc. The students can pick one in turn and then blow up their balloon. They can then describe the shape and colour and also work together in order to use their balloons to decorate the nurture room!

# Beat Boredom!

In this activity the students are asked to consider ways to beat boredom. What could they do? How could they help themselves/ What activities would help them to cope more effectively with this feeling both in and outside of the classroom and who, in particular, might be able to help them in this? Once ideas have been shared amongst the group, students can then design their own individual Beat Boredom strategy sheets on the format provided. They can choose to do simple illustrations or write out a list of top tips as they see fit.

# Bouncy ball Game

The students can be arranged in a circle and given random numbers by the facilitator. If they have problems in remembering their number then this can be provided on a large sticky label to wear on their sleeves. The facilitator then calls out a number and bounces the large soft ball in the centre of the circle. The student with that number runs into the centre and tries to catch the ball before it bounces for a second time. The student then bounces the ball back to the facilitator and the game continues.

**Always finish with Closing Compliments (5 mins)
See Page 18
Try to make some of your own relevant to whatever has happened during the session**

**Section 2: Managing Feelings**

**Session 9**

## THE BAG GAME

**A range of different coloured and shaped balloons e.g.**
Red
Green
Yellow
Gold
Purple
Long
Round
Oval
Large
Small etc

**Section 2: Managing Feelings**

**Session 9**

## BEAT BOREDOM!

This is my advice:

# Section 2: Managing Feelings
# Session 10
# Introduction

The facilitator can reinforce the group rules and present the topic for this session which is feeling different. The students can be asked to thought-storm the following questions: What makes us feel different and how are we different? It may be helpful to provide a few examples such as colour of skin, skills and talents, personality, religious faith, likes and dislikes, physical appearance overall, family makeup and social situation etc. It may be helpful for the facilitator to also ask the students why it is important to respect such differences and not label people in a negative way.

## The Bag Game

The bag is passed around the group containing a range of different coloured and shaped beads e.g. red, green, yellow, gold, silver purple, long, round, oval, square, etc. The students can pick one in turn and then describe the shape and colour and also work together in order to use their beads to create a piece of jewellery. The facilitator can provide string or cord as appropriate and negotiate with the students as to which beads should be threaded in which order so as to create the most attractive necklace or bracelet.

## Different dilemmas

The students are presented with the activity sheet which contains a series of ten situations. Each of these describes someone who is different in some way and may therefore be experiencing some difficulty in being accepted by those who are not the same. They are asked to consider the following 3 questions for each situation:
- What makes this person feel different?
- How do you think they feel?
- What could others do to help them?

## Copy the clap game

The students stand in a circle and the facilitator begins the game by performing a simple action – for example, crouching down and touching the floor. The students all then clap twice and then the facilitator names and points to a student. They then think of a new action to show the rest of the group. The students again clap twice and the performer names and points to another student. The game continues in this way and the aim is to have no hesitation in the flow of the game. This clearly demands concentration and is something that improves with practice.

## Always finish with Closing Compliments (5 mins)
## See Page 18
## Try to make some of your own relevant to whatever has happened during the session

**Section 2: Managing Feelings**

**Session 10**

# THE BAG GAME

**A range of different coloured and shaped beads e.g.**
Red
Green
Yellow
Gold
Silver
Purple
Long
Round
Oval
Square etc

**Section 2: Managing Feelings**

**Session 10**

# DIFFERENT DILEMMAS

Look at the situations below and then answer the following questions about them:

What make this person feel different?
How do you think they feel?
What could other do to help them?

| | |
|---|---|
| 1. Boy in a wheelchair | 2. Blind man at roadside |
| 3. Child left out in playground looking sad | 4. Asian woman in a queue of white people |
| 5. The only black boy in a class | 6. Old woman at bus stop |
| 7. Child with psoriasis | 8. Little girl with hearing aids |
| 9. A fat child looking at others on the football pitch | 10. A man with no legs begging on the street |

# Section 3

## Motivation

# Section 3: Motivation
# Session 1
# Introduction

The facilitator can once again reinforce the group rules for the students prior to engaging them in a circle round. In this activity they are asked to identify things that make them feel happy, that make them want to work, things that they like doing and things that they feel good at. The idea is to reinforce the notion of motivation and the fact that things that motivate us generally make us feel good and want to learn and work and get on with people.

## The Bag Game

The bag is once again passed around the group containing a selection of writing and drawing tools such as a pencil, paintbrush, a biro, a felt-tip etc. Once again the students are encouraged to describe each of these in detail identifying size, shape and what they would specifically be used for.

## My Top Ten Aims

In order to motivate ourselves it is often important to set goals looking to the future and identifying things that we'd really like to do or achieve. The students can write or draw in the boxes provided identifying 10 things that they would really like to do or achieve in the future. They can then identify one of these that they think they can work towards now at this current point in time and also identifying who might help them. It is also important to reinforce the fact that goals and aims can seem rather large and we need to break these down. So students can then be asked to identify the first step that they might take in order to be able to achieve their goals.

## Throwing the Magic Name

In this opening game the first student says the name of another student in the circle. As they say the name, they mime throwing a ball to the student whose name they have just said as if they are 'throwing' the name. The student whose name it is mimes catching it. The second student then says the name of another student and mimes a throw at the same time. This continues for some time and generally results in children saying the names of children they don't often speak to. This can be repeated using a real soft ball.

**Always finish with Closing Compliments (5 mins)
See Page 18
Try to make some of your own relevant to whatever has happened during the session**

**Section 3: Motivation**

**Session 1**

## THE BAG GAME

**A selection of writing and drawing tools:**

Pencil
Paintbrush
Biro
Felt tip pen
Rubber sharpener etc

**Section 3: Motivation**

**Session 1**

## DIFFERENT DILEMMAS

Look to the future! Write or draw ten things that you would really like to do or achieve in the future. Write or draw in the boxes below:

| | |
|---|---|
| 1 | |
| 2 | |
| 3 | |
| 4 | |
| 5 | |
| 6 | |
| 7 | |
| 8 | |
| 9 | |
| 10 | |

**Stop, think and reflect!**

Which on can you work towards now?

Who else can help you?

What are the first three steps you can take?

1.
2.
3.

# Section 3: Motivation
# Session 2
# Introduction

The facilitator can reinforce the group rules prior to engaging the students in a circle round. This can involve reviewing their top 10 aims from the last session. Students can identify their key aim and perhaps articulate the first steps that they might have taken in order to begin to meet this goal. It may then be useful for the facilitator to reinforce the fact that we as human beings can often be motivators of others and we can usually do this by being supportive, friendly and kind. The students can discuss in turn, around the circle, focusing on the following question: 'How can I make others feel positive and happy?'

## The Bag Game

The bag is once again passed around the circle containing a selection of coloured pieces of materials such as checked cotton, felt, velour, ribbon, silk etc. The students are asked to describe each of these in turn, how they feel, how they smell, how they feel against their skin, what they might be used for etc.

## Mighty Motivators

In this activity the students are asked to self-reflect identifying things that make them feel happy, things that make them want to work hard, things that make them want to help others and things that want to make them try something new. It will be important to reinforce the fact that it is often easier to do things in the learning context when we feel confident and happy. What we need to do is to create such situations for ourselves even when things initially seem a little bit hard.

## Fruit Salad

The facilitator assigns different fruit names to each of the pupils in sequence around the circle, for example, apple, pear, banana or lemon. The facilitator then calls out the fruit names in random order and students with the names called are required to stand up and change places. This can be repeated until everyone is sitting on a different chair from the one they originally sat on.

**Always finish with Closing Compliments (5 mins)**
**See Page 18**
**Try to make some of your own relevant to whatever has happened during the session**

**Section 3: Motivation**

**Session 2**

## THE BAG GAME

**Coloured pieces of material:**

Checked cotton
Felt
Velour
Ribbon
Silk
Wool etc

**Section 3: Motivation**

**Session 2**

## MIGHTY MOTIVATORS

Things that make me feel happy

Things that make me want to work hard

Things that make me want to help others

Things that make me want to try something new

# Section 3: Motivation
# Session 3
# Introduction

The facilitator can reinforce the group rules prior to engaging the students in a circle round. S/he will then explain the rules of the Blast Off! game. This involves counting how many people there are in the circle together. This is the number that starts the counting backwards. The students must watch each other carefully. One student must stand and say the highest number. Others must follow one at a time counting backwards. If 2 (or more) students stand up or move to stand up everyone must start again. The game is only complete when they get to 1 and then all must shout 'blast off!'

The game can be repeated and at greater speed as their skills improve.

## The Bag Game

The bag is once again passed around the circle containing a selection of keep fit items or pictures of keep fit activities, e.g. skipping rope, weights, running shoes, a person jogging, a picture of a gymnast etc. The students will take turns to act these out for the other students to then guess what they are doing in order to keep fit.

## How Do I Keep Fit?

The facilitator can then ask the students to put their hands on their hearts or find a pulse. They will then be asked to count the number of beats for a period of 15 seconds. The facilitator can then ask: 'How could they make their heart go faster?' Ideas can then be demonstrated physically. Students can discuss the energetic activities, e.g. skipping, jumping; running. The students can then complete the activity sheet.
Students can finally identify their own motivators for keeping fit and well? What drives them and others and motivates them to do this? How are their motivators similar and different?

**Always finish with Closing Compliments (5 mins)**
**See Page 18**
**Try to make some of your own relevant to whatever has happened during the session**

**Section 3: Motivation**

**Session 3**

**THE BAG GAME**

**Pictures of:**

Skipping rope
Jogger
Weights
Gymnast etc

**Section 3: Motivation**

**Session 3**

These are my pictures of what I think will make my heart go faster

# Section 3: Motivation
# Session 4
# Introduction

At the outset the Group rules can be reinforced with all members of the group. The facilitator will chant with the students the months of the year in order. S/he will then explain the rules of the birthday game. The students will then once again chant the months of the year in order. Students whose birthdays are in that particular month will, get up, run round the circle and back to their original chair. While the student is running the remaining students can count until they are back to their chair and then continue with the months from where they stopped in the sequence.

# The Bag Game

The bag is once again passed around the circle containing cards illustrating all the months of the year. The students can place the months of the year in order without communicating with each other.

The facilitator will then ask the students to put the months into seasons.

# Let's Keep Fit!

The facilitator will ask the students 'What does being fit mean?' The facilitator will ask the students to remember the ideas they may have had during the last session when considering what makes their hearts beat faster.

The facilitator can inform the students that they are going to take part in different activities and monitor what happens to their hearts. Students can find their pulses and the facilitator explain that this is the 'resting heart beat'.

The group can then go out to the playground with their prepared activity sheet and a clipboard and pencil. The students can be encouraged to do a few 'warm up' exercises. Before and at the end of each activity the students will take their pulses while timed for 30secs. Each student can then record this on their prepared activity sheet.

Students can evaluate the effects of each activity and ask why they think it is important for all of us to exercise and what motivates us to take exercise? They can also consider how unhealthy behaviours such as smoking, over eating, taking drugs and not taking exercise may harm people's well being and reduce their motivation.

**Always finish with Closing Compliments (5 mins)**
**See Page 18**
**Try to make some of your own relevant to whatever has happened during the session**

**Section 3: Motivation**

**Session 4**

### THE BAG GAME

**Months of the year**

---

**Section 3: Motivation**

**Session 4**

**Will these activitites make my heart beat faster?**

My resting heart beat is _____ beats in 30 seconds

| Draw or write the activity | My heart beat (in 30 secs) before the activity | My heart beat (in 30 secs) after the activity |
|---|---|---|
|  |  |  |
|  |  |  |
|  |  |  |
|  |  |  |
|  |  |  |

# Section 3: Motivation
# Session 5
# Introduction

At the outset the Group rules can be reinforced with all members of the group. The facilitator can ask the circle of students to describe 1 thing that they have improved on during this week. The students can take turns talking about what they have improved on and the facilitator can encourage and prompt the students to contribute. The facilitator can also write each contribution down for use in the bag game.

## The Bag Game

The bag is once again passed around the circle containing a selection of the achievements identified in the circle introduction game. The students can take it in turns to select one from the bag. They can then describe the achievement and complete the sentence: 'I think ...... did well to achieve this because.....

## Achieving

Each student will be given a 'My achievements' activity sheet Students can then write achievements or draw achievements into the 'book' in the worksheet.

The facilitator can then ask each student to say 'My name is ....... and I have achieved in .............', The next student will then say, 'His name is ..... and he has achieved in ........ and my name is ........ and I have achieved in ......... This can continue until all members of the group have taken part.

The facilitator can then ask the students what they would like to achieve out of school context and ask them to also identify the reasons and motivation for making such choices and setting such goals for themselves.

**Always finish with Closing Compliments (5 mins)**
**See Page 18**
**Try to make some of your own relevant to whatever has happened during the session**

**Section 3: Motivation**

**Session 5**

## THE BAG GAME

**Students own achievements**

**Section 3: Motivation**

**Session 5**

## MY ACHIEVEMENTS

|  |  |
|---|---|
|  |  |
|  |  |

Copyright of the Nurture Group Network 2011

# Section 3: Motivation
# Session 6
# Introduction

At the outset the Group rules can be reinforced with all members of the group. The facilitator can then nominate a leader who can perform various actions in this initial Follow the Leader game, e.g. clapping, hopping etc. When someone performs an incorrect action the game starts again with a different leader. It is repeated to give every child the opportunity to be a leader.

## The Bag Game

The bag is then passed around the circle containing a selection of pictures of the jobs that people do, e.g. police, ambulance, nurse, dentist etc. The students can take it in turns to select one from the bag. They can then describe the job. The students will then be asked what qualities people would need to do each job, e.g. patience, kindness etc.

## Activities

The facilitator can next ask the students how many jobs they think adults do around the school. The students can take it in turns to name the jobs and the people who do those jobs. They can also try to work out what motivates each person in their job. For example, a teacher may enjoy being with young people and gain great pleasure from seeing them learn and develop. The facilitator may wish to make a list of these jobs for a class display.

The facilitator can then ask the students the following questions:
How many of these jobs could the students do? The facilitator can once again make a list for display.

The students will then be provided with a sheet of A4 paper folded into 4. They can then draw and label 4 jobs that they can do that are currently performed by other people.

## Can I be a leader?

The facilitator will ask the students if they have ever experienced taking on the role of a leader. e.g. football captain, group lead in class etc. Students can discuss these leading roles, the qualities and the responsibilities needed for them. They can also consider the question: what motivates someone to want to be the leader?

They can then create a flag or a scroll to represent a leadership role that children can take (Example 'I can be a leader').

## Always finish with Closing Compliments (5 mins)
## See Page 18
## Try to make some of your own relevant to whatever has happened during the session

Section 3: Motivation

Session 6

## THE BAG GAME

**Pictures of people who have well known jobs**

Farmer
Police person
Ambulance person
Nurse
Dentist
Fire person
Doctor etc

Section 3: Motivation

Session 6

## I CAN BE A LEADER

# Section 3: Motivation
# Session 7
# Introduction Game

At the outset the Group rules can be reinforced with all members of the group. The facilitator can ensure that the group sit in a circle. The facilitator can explain that all the student's will take turns to call out another student's name when they have done that they will need to swap seats with the said student. This can be repeated and the facilitator can ensure that every student has a turn.

## The Bag Game

The facilitator can then tell a fable with a moral e.g. The Tortoise and the Hare. The students will discuss the story and its moral to show understanding of what a moral means. The bag is then passed around the circle and contains a selection of pictures that illustrate a fable with a moral. The students can take it in turns to select one from the bag. They can then place the pictures in order to sequence the fable. The students will then retell the fable they have created and attempt the articulate the associated moral.

## Main Activities

The facilitator can next discuss with the students how to recognise what each individual does when s/he is frustrated. Ideas can be recorded by the facilitator on the white board as they say them.

The facilitator can then encourage discussion regarding how exercise can release anger and stress. The group will discuss different types of exercise and talk about their favourite types of exercise. Which exercises are appropriate to let out anger and why do they think this might be the case?

Students can then create their own posters about how exercise can release anger, stress and frustration.

They can then focus upon the following question: what motivates great sportsmen and women to keep trying and training? Is it the winning? Is it the feeling of success? Is it the reward of people admiring them? If they were in such shoes, what do they think would motivate them?

**Always finish with Closing Compliments (5 mins)**
**See Page 18**
**Try to make some of your own relevant to whatever has happened during the session**

**Section 3: Motivation**

**Session 7**

**THE BAG GAME**

Pictures that form the sequence of The Hare and the Tortoise

# Section 3: Motivation
# Session 8
# Introduction Game

The facilitator can reinforce the group rules prior to engaging the students in a circle round. The facilitator introduces the circle game as 'Dracula'!
A student is nominated to be Dracula. She says a victim's name and starts to walk towards them and the victim must then say another's name in order to change the victim. The 'Dracula' then changes direction towards the new victim. If a victim is caught (because they haven't said another victim's name in time), they become Dracula.

## The Bag Game

The bag is once again passed around the circle containing a 'ticket' with each student's name on. The students can take it turns to take out a ticket and they can also take it in turns to say a positive thing about the student they have picked.

## What does motivation mean?

The facilitator can then ask if the students know what motivation means, making reference to work undertaken in previous sessions. The group can discuss this and make their suggestions in order to attempt to jointly agree a group definition for motivation.

The facilitator can then ask the group if they can name the different people who can help them and keep them motivated both in and out of school when they have a problem.

## Activity Sheet

The facilitator can then read the letter entitled 'Dear Dallas', stopping at certain points to ask the group how they would feel in this situation and to elicit their views.

The students can fill out the 'problem resolver' together as a group (pin it up and write on it). The facilitator can talk about the fact that helping to resolve/solve other people's problems means that you have respect and you care for them. This is also a mark of friendship and shows that we genuinely care for and empathise with each other.

The facilitator can then pose the following questions:
'What can you do to show respect for others'?
'What do others do to show respect and care for you'?
The students will then complete activity sheet which requires them to identify and record 5 good reasons to be motivated and to get out of bed in the morning. It may be helpful to provide students with some time to share their ideas.

## Always finish with Closing Compliments (5 mins)
## See Page 18
## Try to make some of your own relevant to whatever has happened during the session

Section 3: Motivation

Session 8

## THE BAG GAME

'Tickets' with each student's name on

---

Section 3: Motivation

Session 8

## PROBLEM RESOLVER

1. What is the problem?
_____
_____
_____
_____

2. How is the person feeling?
_____
_____
_____
_____

3. What could the person do?
i _____
ii _____
iii _____

4. Which solution is the best and why?
_____
_____
_____
_____

5. How will the person know that their peoblem has been resolved?
_____
_____
_____
_____

---

Section 3: Motivation

Session 8

## DEAR DALLAS LETTER

Dear Dallas,

Hi my name is Daniel and I used to have a really good relationship with my big sister Claire. I am 9 next week and she is now 14 and she doesn't really speak to me any more.

She used to take me shopping and swimming at the weekends and other fun stuff, but she doesn't any more.

Claire says everything is boring and she can't be bothered to do anything with me. Dad said that she needs motivating but I don't know how to do that.

I really miss how my sister used to be, what can I do to get her back?

Please help,

Daniel

---

Section 3: Motivation

Session 8

## GET UP AND GO!

Getting motivated! Can you think of 5 good reasons to get you our of bed and motivated.

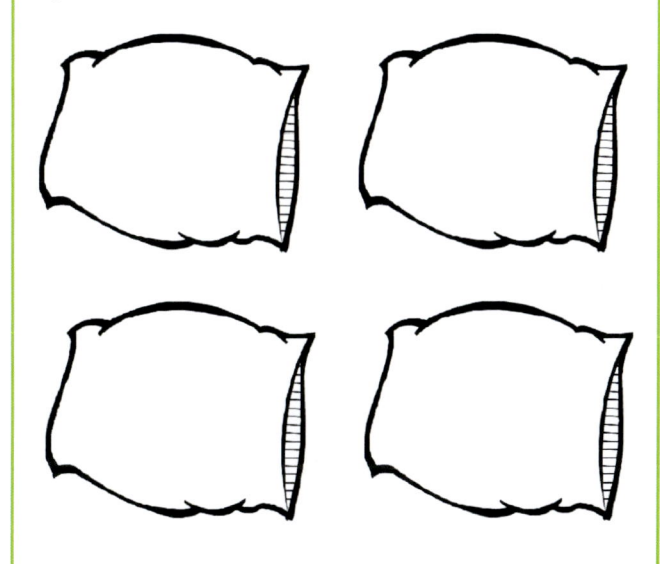

Discuss your ideas with a friend and record them in these pillows.

# Section 3: Motivation
# Session 9
# Introduction

The facilitator can reinforce the group rules prior to engaging the students in a circle round. The facilitator can then make the statement ' If I were a colour, I would be … because…'. e.g. If I were a colour I would be yellow because I feel happy and sunny today! The group can discuss the statement. Each student will then repeat the statement with their own ideas and choice of colour.

## The Bag Game

The bag is then passed around the circle containing a selection of coloured shapes, e.g. black, red, blue, purple etc. The students can take it in turns to say the colour and describe what the colour reminds them of e.g. This is the colour yellow. It reminds me of daffodils. Each student can expand upon their ideas by saying why it reminds them of a certain thing, time or place.

## Activities
## Creating a challenge and a goal
## Can I teach a skill? Can I learn a new skill?

The students will already have been asked before this session to have identified a skill that they are good at, that they can teach another student or the group as a whole.

Each student will then take it in turns to demonstrate their skill. The other students will then be given time to question the student and decide if they want to learn the skill. The facilitator can then pair the students up. The students can be given time to teach their partner the skill. The group can then come together and each pair can show the rest of the group the new skill they have learnt.

Each student will then complete an activity sheet identifying how motivated they felt as they taught the skill to another person and how they felt when learning a new skill.

**Always finish with Closing Compliments (5 mins)**
**See Page 18**
**Try to make some of your own relevant to whatever has happened during the session**

**Section 3: Motivation**

**Session 9**

## THE BAG GAME

**Different colours shapes:**

Blue
Black
Red
Purple
Yellow etc

**Section 3: Motivation**

**Session 9**

## CAN I TEACH A SKILL?

What is your skill?

Who were teaching?

How did it make you feel to see this person performing the skill you had taught them?

# Section 3: Motivation
# Session 10
# Introduction

The facilitator can reinforce the group rules prior to engaging the students in a circle round. The facilitator can direct all the students to close their eyes and listen for 2 minutes. The facilitator can time the 2 minutes.

The students can then take it in turns to say what sounds they heard during this period of time. These sounds can be written down on cards ready for the bag game by the facilitator/students as appropriate.

## The Bag Game

The bag is then passed around the circle containing cards with all the 'sounds' that students listed during the introductory activity. The students can then take it in turns to take a card. They will then take it in turns to talk about the sound and attempt to describe it in detail.

## Activities
## Going for Gold!

The facilitator can ask the question: When you grow up, what would you like to be? The students can discuss jobs and what each of them aspires to and why.

The facilitator will then pose the question: What will you need to do in order to achieve this? The idea here is to reinforce the fact that in order to achieve our goal we not only have to stay motivated but we also have to set realistic targets which we can achieve on the way. If we see ourselves succeeding on a step by step basis then this will help us to stay motivated on the journey to reaching and meeting our goals.

## Activity Sheet

Using the information from the previous activity the students can complete the activity sheet 'Going for Gold'. The facilitator may leave any notes on display for the students to use to enable them to complete the worksheet.

It may also be helpful for students to work in pairs with a Motivational Buddy who can support them in identifying the steps that they can take along the way.

**Always finish with Closing Compliments (5 mins)**
**See Page 18**
**Try to make some of your own relevant to whatever has happened during the session**

Section 3: Motivation

Session 10

## THE BAG GAME

**The cares in the bag will have the sounds of the noises the boys heard during the introduction**

---

Section 3: Motivation

Session 10

## GOING FOR GOLD!
## WHEN I GROW UP I WANT TO BE:

Steps I can take to achieve this:
_____
_____
_____

# Section 4

## Empathy

# Section 4: Empathy
# Session 1
# Introduction

The facilitator can reinforce the group rules prior to engaging the students in a circle round. This involves all of them in making a feelings face. They can choose or identify their own feeling and mime this to the rest of the group. Each member of the group has to try and guess what that feeling is that's being represented by each of the individual students.

## The Bag Game

The bag is once again passed around the circle containing a selection of coloured plastic shapes. The students are asked to describe each of these in turn, how they feel, how they smell, the number of sides/points, what they might be used for etc.

## Friends are Caring and Sharing

In this activity students are asked to write and draw in the star shapes provided on the format identifying ways in which they care for others. How is it that they show others that they are or can be a good friend?

## The Noisy Game

The students are labelled A and B alternately around the circle. The A's are asked to tell their partner B about, for example, their favourite food, hobby, pop group, football team or pop idol. Initially the B's do not listen to the A's and they make as much noise as they possibly can such as calling out to their friends across the circle. The facilitator then calls for silence – it may be helpful to have agreed a signal for this prior to the start of the activity. The A's then talk to the B's again and this time the B's are asked to listen extremely well, nodding their heads and smiling at appropriate points and making comments as appropriate. The idea here is to reinforce the fact that if you don't listen you can't hear, but there is also no point in speaking if you are not being listened to. It may also be useful to ask the children how they felt when they weren't being listened to appropriately and to ask those who were making the noise how they think the other person may have felt, thus re-introducing the concept of empathy.

**Always finish with Closing Compliments (5 mins)**
**See Page 18**
**Try to make some of your own relevant to whatever has happened during the session**

Section 4: Empathy

Session 1

## THE BAG GAME

**Plastic 3d shapes:**

Triangle
Hexagon
Circle
Square
Tectangle
Cube etc

---

Section 4: Empathy

Session 1

## FRIENDS ARE CARING AND SHARING

Write and/or draw in the star shapes. How do we show that we care for others? How do we show them that we are 'good' friends?

# Section 4: Empathy
# Session 2
# Introduction

The facilitator can reinforce the group rules once again prior to asking the students to engage in a circle round activity. This involves making actions which each individual has to copy in turn around the group. Each of the students can then take turns in instigating this game. This may involve making a range of different actions such as clapping, jumping up and down, skipping, hopping etc.

## The Bag Game

The bag is once again passed around the circle containing a selection of toy cars or means of transport such as a car, a lorry, a fire engine, a train etc. The students can describe each of these in turn and also identify the ways in which they might be used in the real world.

## The Card Activity and Using the Problem Solving Sheet

In this activity students are presented with a series of cards identifying a range of people in difficult or complex situations in which they are feeling upset or distressed. For example, a picture of a boy being bullied by two other boys, a picture of a girl on her own watching others playing, a picture of an old lady being mugged at the bus stop etc. The facilitator can then ask individuals to consider how they would feel if they were in each of these situations prior to presenting the problem solving sheet. This is a stepped process for problem solving. It may be useful for the facilitator to model this initially by choosing one of the situation cards and talking through each of the five steps in turn identifying the problems: who might help, what strategies the person could use, what the best option would be and how that person would know that the problem was then solved.

## Plasticine Statues

This activity emphasises how important it is for the students to look at body language and to begin to recognise how people feel or may be feeling from the way they stand and move. Pupils are put into pairs around the circle and labelled A and B. The A's are told to stand up and look like aggressive/angry statues. Once all the A's have become cross statues, their partners can walk silently around the circle looking at the gallery of cross statues. Then the facilitator can ask each of the B's to remodel the statues into something gentle and calm. Once they have been remodelled the B's can again walk around the circle and notice the difference in the statues.

### Always finish with Closing Compliments (5 mins)
### See Page 18
### Try to make some of your own relevant to whatever has happened during the session

Section 4: Empathy

Session 2

# THE BAG GAME

**Toys car/means of transport:**

Car
Lorry
Fire engine
Train
Bue etc

---

Section 4: Empathy

Session 2

# THE CARD ACTIVITY

| Picture of boy being bullied by two others | Picture of girl on her own watching others play |
|---|---|
| Picture of an old lady being mugged at the bus stop | Picture of little boy in the supermarket who is lost |
| Picture of girl looking at a friend who has a new mobile phone - she doesnt have one | Picture of boy being sent off the pitch for a foul in the football match |

---

Section 4: Empathy

Session 2

# THE PROBLEM SOLVING SHEET

1. What is the problem/ How does the person feel?


2. Who might help? What could they do?


3. What strategies can the person use?
   Option 1
   Option 2
   Option 3

4. The best is option _____ because



5. How will the person know that the problem is solved? What will be different?

# Section 4: Empathy
# Session 3
# Introduction

The facilitator can reinforce the group rules prior to engaging the students in 'The Clapping Game'. This involves going around the circle making use of a variety of different rhythms which each student in turn has to copy. The facilitator can then focus on the empathy skills displayed within the group, posing the question, 'Are they understanding of each other when they make a mistake and how do they know how someone else feels in this situation? Can they put themselves in the other person's shoes?' This session is a follow on from session 2 so the facilitator may wish to recap upon the previous session.

## The Bag Game

The bag is once again passed around the circle containing a selection of different pictures of different 'problems' e.g. bullying, isolation etc. The students can describe each one in turn making reference to the 'problem' in the picture and how they might be able to solve it. What could they do? Who would be best placed to help them?

## What is a problem?

In this activity the students are asked to discuss what is a problem? Also, how can we as friends help people deal with problems? The facilitator may want to write their ideas on the board as these are articulated. Once this is completed the students can be asked if they can think of a problem in or out of school that as a group they could come up with a solution for. The facilitator may wish to prepare an example in order to prompt the students in this task.

**Dear . . . . . .**

The facilitator can next discuss the problems on the activity sheets with the group. The students can firstly identify the problem then together come up with solutions. At this point the facilitator can write the students ideas onto the board – leaving them there to aid the students with the completion of their activity sheets.

## Always finish with Closing Compliments (5 mins)
## See Page 18
## Try to make some of your own relevant to whatever has happened during the session

Section 4: Empathy

Session 3

## THE BAG GAME

**Pictures of different problems**

---

Section 4: Empathy

Session 3

## PROBLEM SOLVING

Dear Karen,

Some people who live near me are being really nasty to me. They call me spotty and fat. It makes me feel so unhappy. Can you help?

From Patrick

Dear Patrick,
_____
_____
_____
_____
_____

From Karen

Dear Karen,

My friend's brother is smoking and he is only 12. I saw him and he told me if I told anyone that he would get me. Please can you help me.

From Sheila

Dear Sheila,
_____
_____
_____
_____
_____

From Karen

---

Section 4: Empathy

Session 3

## PROBLEM SOLVING

Dear Karen,

Some people who live near me are being really nasty to me. They call me spotty and fat. It makes me feel so unhappy. Can you help?

From Patrick

How would this make you feel?

How could you help?

Dear Karen,

My friend's brother is smoking and he is only 12. I saw him and he told me if I told anyone that he would get me. Please can you help me.

From Sheila

How would this make you feel?

How could you help?

# Section 4: Empathy
# Session 4
# Introduction

The facilitator can reinforce the group rules prior to engaging the students in a circle round. The facilitator discusses with the group what a positive comment is. This requires all of them making a positive comment about the student on their right in the circle. Afterwards the student receiving the positive comment will say how it makes them feel to receive such a positive comment.

# The Bag Game

The bag is once again passed around the circle containing a selection of positive and negative comments. The students are asked to describe each of these in turn, and how it would make them feel if this was said to them. It may be useful for the facilitator to highlight similarities and differences in the student's responses.

# Activity
# On a Positive Note

Each student will next receive a sheet containing ten positive statements. The students can cut out the statements and one will be given to each person in the group. Statements can be given on the basis of suitability for each student. Some of the students may need help with reading them and the facilitator will need to be sensitive to this. While the students decide which statement to give to which person they will be asked not to talk to each other.

The students can then come back together and sit in a circle and discuss (facilitator led) how it felt to receive positive comments and how it felt to give somebody else positive comments. They could also discuss whether the comments they received were all the same or if they were a mixture.

**Always finish with Closing Compliments (5 mins)
See Page 18
Try to make some of your own relevant to whatever has happened during the session**

## Section 4: Empathy
Session 4

### THE BAG GAME

A selection of positive and negative comments

---

## Section 4: Empathy
Session 4

### PROBLEM SOLVING

You are always kind

You are very tidy

You always share

You have a nice smile

You look out for me

You help people

You are good at reading

You are good at maths

You are always happy

You are funny

---

## Section 4: Empathy
Session 4

### ON A POSITIVE NOTE

Kind

Tidy

Share

Smile

Look out for me

Help

---

## Section 4: Empathy
Session 4

### ON A POSITIVE NOTE

Reading

Maths

Happy

Funny

# Section 4: Empathy
# Session 5
# Introduction

The facilitator can reinforce the group rules prior to engaging the students in a circle round. This involves all of them thinking of an object that moves, and then being asked to mime/act out this object to the group who are required to guess what it is.

## The Bag Game

The bag is once again passed around the circle containing a selection of toys that can move e.g. a car, a tractor, a train, a snake, a lion, a turtle etc. The students are asked to mime how they think this object would move. The students can then discuss whether they agree if the object would move in this way, if they disagree then they must show how they think it moves

## Activities
## Move like a . . . . . . . .

At this point the students can draw and colour a picture (on the activity sheet provided) of something that they like which moves.

## The Move like a . . . . . . . Game

The facilitator will recap on the bag game conducted at the start of the session and the group can pick a selection of different things that move. The facilitator can write these on the board as they are identified. Then the group can then move into some space. The facilitator can then call out something that moves and they can all mime this animal/object in the room. Then the facilitator can call out another object, and repeat the process.

**Always finish with Closing Compliments (5 mins)**
**See Page 18**
**Try to make some of your own relevant to whatever has happened during the session**

**Section 4: Empathy**

**Session 5**

# THE BAG GAME

**Toys:**

Car
Tractor
Train
Snake
Lion
Turtle

**Section 4: Empathy**

**Session 5**

# Section 4: Empathy
# Session 6
# Introduction

The facilitator can reinforce the group rules once again prior to asking the students to engage in a circle round activity. This involves each child saying something they know about somebody else in the room that they didn't know when they first met them. The facilitator can point out that it is possible to spend a lot of time with people and still not know everything about them. The students may wish to discuss the reasons why this may be the case.

# The Bag Game

The bag is once again passed around the circle containing a selection of items or pictures that specifically relate to the pupils in the group i.e. if a pupil likes Dr. Who then you could put a picture or place a model of the object in the bag. The students then try and guess who the item or picture relates to within the group.

# Activities
# I Know Something You Don't Know

During this activity the students can wander around the room and when they meet another student they are asked to whisper a fact about themselves to that person i.e. favourite colour/game/food, how many brothers sisters they have. . . . .
The facilitator will ask the students to try to remember these facts as they may need to use them in the subsequent Silhouette activity.

# Silhouette

This activity may highlight how much/little the group of students know about each other.
The facilitator will need to turn the lights out and get each student in turn to kneel next to the board. A piece of black paper will be on the board, and another student will be asked to hold up a torch to create the silhouette. The facilitator can then draw around the shadow in pencil. The facilitator can do this for every student in the group. Each child will pick a silhouette to write about. Then they will write or type (using the activity sheet provided) some facts about that student – without using their names.

When this is completed the students can gather back into a circle and in turn say, "I know something you don't know, this person has 2 sisters and likes toffee. . . . . . . . . etc". They will hold up the silhouette while they say this and the other students will try and work out who the person is.

**Always finish with Closing Compliments (5 mins)**
**See Page 18**
**Try to make some of your own relevant to whatever has happened during the session**

**Section 4: Empathy**

**Session 6**

# THE BAG GAME

**Items that specifically relate to person in the group:**

**Scotion 4: Empathy**

**Session 6**

| This person likes |
| This person enjoys |
| This person is good at |
| This person has |

| This person likes |
| This person enjoys |
| This person is good at |
| This person has |

Copyright of the Nurture Group Network 2011

# Section 4: Empathy
# Session 7
# Introduction

The facilitator can reinforce the group rules once again prior to asking the students to engage in a circle round activity. During this activity the chairs will be in a circle and the students and facilitators will stand The aim of the activity is that everyone will end up in their seat. Each person must sit down. If 2 or more people move at once then everyone must stand up again. Although this sounds easy, as the students are not allowed to talk, there is no discussion as to who is going to move and when. This therefore demands a great deal of concentration from all involved.

# The Bag Game

The bag is once again passed around the circle containing a selection of pictures of classroom items. Each card will have the item on it and a list of words that the student cannot use to describe it. The facilitator may want to present an example with the students. For example, the card may say Computer but they may not be allowed to say keyboard, mouse, screen etc to describe the computer. This means that they will have to be extremely selective and creative in the language they use in order to help the rest of the group identify the item.

# Activities
# Dear Dallas

In this activity students can discuss as a group the different people who can help you in school if you have a problem. The facilitator can then read the Dear Dallas letter to the whole group, stopping at certain points to ask them how they would feel if they were in this persons' shoes. The Problem Resolver can be completed by the group with the facilitator acting as a scribe. The facilitator may want to enlarge it onto A3 paper, pin it on the board or wall.

# Respecting and Caring

The facilitator can prompt students to discuss helping people with problems and how, if they do this for someone, then they probably care and respect them. The facilitator can ask the students what they can do to show they care and respect for others. The facilitator will write the ideas that the students come up with onto the board.

Each student can then write their ideas onto the raindrops activity sheet provided.

**Always finish with Closing Compliments (5 mins)**
**See Page 18**
**Try to make some of your own relevant to whatever has happened during the session**

Section 4: Empathy

Session 7

## THE BAG GAME

**Classroom objects cards eg:**

Computer
Board
Felt Pen

---

Section 4: Empathy

Session 7

## PROBLEM RESOLVER

1. What is the problem?
_____
_____
_____
_____

2. How is the person feeling?
_____
_____
_____
_____

3. What could the person do?
i _____
ii _____
iii _____

4. Which solution is the best and why?
_____
_____
_____
_____

5. How will the person know that their peoblem has been resolved?
_____
_____
_____
_____

---

Section 4: Empathy

Session 7

## DEAR DALLAS LETTER

Dear Dallas,

Hi, My name is Simon and I have just moved house to a town where I don't know anyone. My Dad had to move for his work and I hate it here. You see it's not just because I don't know anyone it's also because I am black and there aren't many people round here that are.

At my new school I am the only black person in my class and one of very few in the whole school. People laugh at me and call me names. They don't seem to understand that black is just the colour of my skin underneath I am just the same as them.

I don't want to trouble my Mum and Dad with this as they are very busy and seem to work a lot more down here. I have a good relationship with my Nan but she is too far away now.

Please help,
Simon

---

Section 4: Empathy

Session 7

## RESPECTING AND CARING

How can we and others show that we care for and respect people?

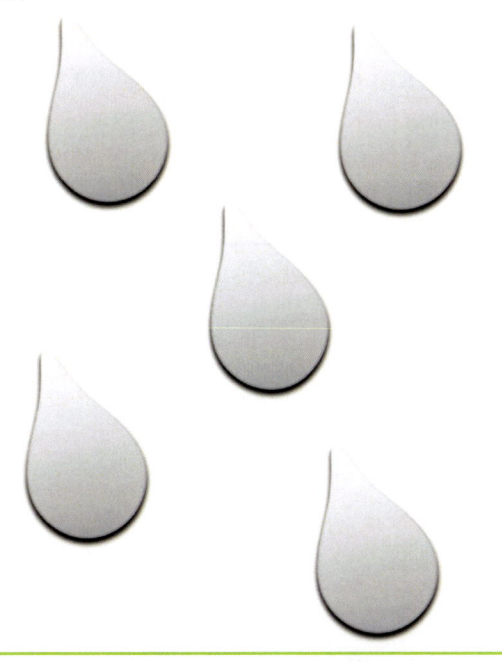

# Section 4: Empathy
# Session 8
# Introduction

The facilitator can reinforce the group rules once again prior to asking the students to engage in a circle round activity. The facilitator can then recap on the contents of session 7 which ties in neatly with session 8. This activity aids the empathetic values of caring and sharing. The facilitator can place a piece of A3 paper on the floor with 2 pens and ask that the students design a poster on the topic of caring and sharing. The facilitator can then observe how the students resolve the problem of having only 2 pens and how they work together as a group.

## The Bag Game

The bag is then passed around the group in which the facilitator will have placed pictures of things you can share e.g. chocolate, cake, books, toys building bricks etc. The students can pick a piece of paper out in turn and discuss why they think that picture is in the bag. And the facilitator can pose the questions can you share this item? Who could you share it with?

## Activities
## Dear Dallas

The students can discuss as a group how it feels when people don't share with you, or someone you are close to isn't as friendly as they were previously. The facilitator can read the Dear Dallas letter to the whole group, stopping at certain points to ask the students how they would feel if they found themselves in this person's shoes. They can then complete the Problem Resolver as a group (This can be enlarged onto A3 paper), and pinned on the board or wall.

## Caring and Sharing

The facilitator can encourage the students to discuss the importance of helping people with problems and how, if you do that for someone you probably care for them. The facilitator can ask the students what they can do to show they still care for others. The facilitator will write the ideas that the students come up with on the board.
Each student can then write their ideas onto the raindrops sheet provided.

**Always finish with Closing Compliments (5 mins)
See Page 18
Try to make some of your own relevant to whatever has happened during the session**

Section 4: Empathy

Session 8

## THE BAG GAME

**Items you could share eg:**

Chocolate
Toys
Books

---

Section 4: Empathy

Session 8

## PROBLEM RESOLVER

1. What is the problem?
_____
_____
_____
_____

2. How is the person feeling?
_____
_____
_____
_____

3. What could the person do?
i _____
ii _____
iii _____

4. Which solution is the best and why?
_____
_____
_____
_____

5. How will the person know that their peoblem has been resolved?
_____
_____
_____
_____

---

Section 4: Empathy

Session 8

## DEAR DALLAS LETTER

Dear Dallas,

Hi my name is Rosie and I go to a lovely school where all the teachers are kind and always listen to you. They never get angry and they never shout.

Me and my best friend Roger went to an after school club and were taught to cook. Roger loves it and I don't so much. Roger has been chosen to take part in a small competition as he is very good and likes to create his own dishes. I am not jealous at all as Roger deserves it and is far better at cooking than me, I don't really enjoy it.

It's just he has made lots of new friends in the club and gets on with them very well. He is also spending much more time with them preparing for the competition. He is not nasty to me or anything like that I just don't see him as much and I miss him.

Please help,
Rosie

---

Section 4: Empathy

Session 8

## CARING AND SHARING

How can we and others show that we care for and respect people? How can we be good friends and share with out friends?

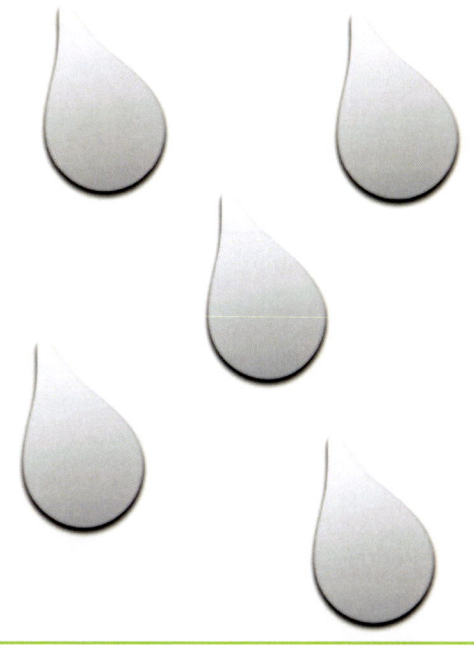

# Section 4: Empathy
# Session 9
# Introduction

The facilitator can reinforce the group rules once again prior to asking the students to engage in a circle round activity. The group can sit in a circle on chairs and discuss what they think a dilemma is. The facilitator can record their ideas on the board as they are articulated. Then the facilitator can ask the group if they or anyone they know has ever been in a dilemma and how they solved it or helped someone to solve their dilemma.

# The Bag Game

The bag is then passed around the group in which the facilitator will have placed pictures of people performing actions to help someone in a dilemma. The students can each pick a piece of paper out of the bag and discuss what they think is going on in the picture and how this behaviour would help somebody to solve their dilemma.

# Activities
# Dealing with Dilemmas

The facilitator can then present and discuss the activity sheets and explain each of the dilemmas in turn. The facilitator can ask the students to firstly identify the dilemma then come up with some solutions. The facilitator can record these ideas on the board to aid students when it comes to recording their responses and ideas on the activity sheet. They can then complete the activity sheets.

# Understanding Others Feelings

The facilitator can next gather the group into a circle and discuss how it makes you feel to help other people who are experiencing difficulties. How does it feel to know that others people also suffer from dilemmas and different dilemmas to perhaps yourself?

**Always finish with Closing Compliments (5 mins)
See Page 18
Try to make some of your own relevant to whatever has happened during the session**

Section 4: Empathy

Session 9

## THE BAG GAME

**Actions that help people during a dilemma eg:**

Hugging
Listening
Smiling

---

Section 4: Empathy

Session 9

## DEALING WITH DILEMMAS AND UNDERSTANDING OTHERS FEELINGS

1. Your friend is cheating at a game and you see them, how could you deal with this?

1.

2.

2. Someone is bullying your friend, how could you help with this?

1.

2.

3. You break one of your mum's/carers' special ornaments, how could you deal with this?

1.

2.

4. You've been invited to 2 friend's parties on the same day, how could you deal with this?

1.

2.

---

Section 4: Empathy

Session 9

## DEALING WITH DILEMMAS AND UNDERSTANDING OTHERS FEELINGS

What are the different ways you could deal with these dilemmas? Think about the differences your advice could make.

Your friend is cheating at a game?

Someone is bullying your friend

You have been invited to 2 parties at the same time

# Section 4: Empathy
# Session 10
# Introduction

The facilitator can reinforce the group rules once again prior to asking the students to engage in a circle round activity. The facilitator can ask the students how we recognise when people are feeling angry. The facilitator can record their suggestions on the board then ask the students if they can think of a time when they noticed someone was angry.

## The Bag Game

The bag game will then be circulated around the group. The facilitator can place some objects in the bag that are perceived to be calming in nature i.e. a book, a pillow, a game etc. Each student will pick out an item and discuss this with the group. They can state whether or not this item would calm them when they are angry and clarify 'If it wouldn't, why wouldn't it?'

## Friends Anger

The facilitator can prompt the students to discuss the different signs that show us people are angry. Then the facilitator can present the activity sheets to the group and record their ideas and responses on the board as they are articulated. This should prompt the thinking and aid completion of the task.

**Always finish with Closing Compliments (5 mins)**
**See Page 18**
**Try to make some of your own relevant to whatever has happened during the session**

**Section 4: Empathy**

**Session 10**

# THE BAG GAME

**Things that calm eg:**

A book
A pillow
Games

---

**Section 4: Empathy**

**Session 10**

# ANGER INDICATOR

Draw and label a picture of an angry person. Show how you know they are angry.

How do you know when your teacher is angry?
_____
_____

How do you know when your friend is angry?
_____
_____

What can you do to help them?
_____
_____

---

**Section 4: Empathy**

**Session 10**

# ANGER INDICATOR

Are these faces angry and how do you know?

# Section 5

## Social Skills

# Section 5: Social Skills
# Session 1
# Introduction

The facilitator can reinforce the group rules prior to engaging the students in 'The Clapping Game'. This involves going around the circle making use of a variety of different rhythms which each student in turn has to copy. The facilitator can then focus on the conceptive social skills posing the question, 'What are social skills?' It may be useful to prompt discussion by identifying some of these such as turn taking, listening, playing well, understanding how others feel, sharing and appropriate use of voice in a range of contexts etc.

## The Bag Game

The bag is once again passed around the circle containing a selection of different coloured marbles and balls. The students can describe each one in turn making reference to colour, shape, size etc.

## Self-reflection Activity

In this activity the students are asked to self-reflect identifying a specific range of social skills and rating themselves on a scale of 1-10 against each one (1 being not too good, 5 being ok and 10 being brilliant). They are finally asked to identify one specific target or area for themselves: what is it that they would like to develop further?

## Wink-wink

An additional chair is placed into the circle and the student sitting next to the empty chair is asked to wink at someone on the other side of the circle. The student who has been winked at then crosses the circle in silence and is required to wink at someone else across the circle and they are then required to sit in the empty chair. This is done as fast as possible until all the pupils are reasonably well mixed up in the circle.

**Always finish with Closing Compliments (5 mins)**
**See Page 18**
**Try to make some of your own relevant to whatever has happened during the session**

**Section 5: Social Skills**

**Session 1**

## THE BAG GAME

**Different coloured marbles and balls**

**Section 5: Social Skills**

**Session 1**

## SELF-REFLECTION ACTIVITY

**My Skills**
Rate on scale 1-10
(1 = not too good, 5 = okay, 10 = brilliant)

**Turn Taking**

| 1 | 2 | 3 | 4 | 5 | 6 | 7 | 8 | 9 | 10 |

**Good Looking**

| 1 | 2 | 3 | 4 | 5 | 6 | 7 | 8 | 9 | 10 |

**Good Listening**

| 1 | 2 | 3 | 4 | 5 | 6 | 7 | 8 | 9 | 10 |

**Caring for Others**

| 1 | 2 | 3 | 4 | 5 | 6 | 7 | 8 | 9 | 10 |

**What can I improve?**
**Set one target**
**My social skills target is**

# Section 5: Social Skills
# Session 2
# Introduction

The facilitator can reinforce the group rules prior to asking the students to articulate their social skills target set in the previous session. They can then ask students to nominate people from the group who have listened well, been kind, taken turns or shared etc i.e. those who have developed and shown good or appropriate social skills during the intervening period.

## The Bag Game

The bag is once again passed around the group containing a selection of toy animals such as a goat, a zebra, a cat, a dog and an elephant etc. Once again the students can be encouraged to describe each of these in turn identifying shape, size, colour and where they might see each of these animals.

## In Control

In this activity sheet the students are introduced to the concept of focus of control. The idea here is to reinforce the fact that we all need to be in control and take responsibility for our own behaviour as blaming others won't help us to change or succeed. Students are presented with a series of boxes – they are asked to read through these and decide if each person in each of the situations is actually taking responsibility for their behaviour or are they blaming others. For example, I missed the goal because James shouted at me just as I was about to kick it – is reflective of someone who is not taking responsibility or being in control; they are simply blaming others. It may be useful for the facilitator to model this response and to also talk through each of these in turn with the students.

## Circle Warm Up

As for all subsequent sessions, the students will be seated in the circle ready to start the session. In the initial warm-up the students are asked to change places in the circle if, for example:

- You have laces in your shoes
- You like Busted
- You like playing football
- You like eating fruit
- You hate vegetables
- You love vegetables
- You like chocolate

The reasons for changing places can be varied by the facilitator as appropriate.

**Always finish with Closing Compliments (5 mins)
See Page 18
Try to make some of your own relevant to whatever has happened during the session**

Section 5: Social Skills

Session 2

## THE BAG GAME

**A selection of toy animals:**

Zebra
Goat
Dog
Cat
Elephant etc

Section 5: Social Skills

Session 2

## IN CONTROL

We all need to be in control and take responsibility for our own behaviour – blaming others won't help us to change or succeed.

Look at the statements in the boxes. Next decide if the person is in control and taking responsibility or if they re blaming others.

Colour code the boxes green=in control, red=blaming others.

| | | |
|---|---|---|
| I missed the goal because James shouted at me just as I was about to kick it. | I got told off because my friends made me muck about in class | My mum shouted at me so I kicked the Hoover and it broke. |
| I got one hour detention because the teacher doesn't like me. | The teacher was in a bad mood so I ran out of the room. | He made me punch him because he gave me a funny look. |
| I didn't do well in the maths test because the teacher made it too hard. | I learnt all my spellings so I got 10/10 in the test. | I tripped up because I wasn't looking where I was going. |

# Section 5: Social Skills
# Session 3
# Introduction

The facilitator can reinforce the group rules prior to engaging the students in the 'Clap and change' activity. This involves going around the circle in turns. Each student must clap either once or twice. One clap means they should continue in the same direction and two claps means they should change direction. The facilitator can then focus on the concept of social skills posing the question, 'How well can you observe others and react?' This activity involves turn taking, watching carefully, playing well, understanding how others react slower than others etc.

# The Bag Game

The bag is once again passed around the circle containing a selection of cards that depict different types of sport. The students can describe their picture without labelling or naming the sport and the other students must attempt to guess the sport. The facilitator can emphasise the need to look, listen and take turns appropriately in this activity

# Friendship Activity

In this activity the students are asked to reflect over the last few days and focus on one thing that they feel they have improved upon. Each student can take turns to inform the rest of the group of their improvement. Each student can then be given a 'sweet' (card cut into sweet shapes) and each will write on the 'sweet' an achievement. The 'sweets' will then be handed to each students in turn. Students can then reflect on how they all felt when they were given the sweets.

# Activities
# 'Helping Friends'

The students can be placed into pairs and each pair given a role play card. Students can then take it turns to act out the problem or situation described on the card. The remainder of the students will then attempt to identify a solution for the problem.

Students can then discuss how good it is to help a friend and how it feels to be helped and also think about how important it is to really listen to others when they are describing their problems and / asking for help.

Each student can then be provided with an activity sheet with a 'friend' in the class/group/school. They can write down the characteristics that make a good friend around the 'friend'.

**Always finish with Closing Compliments (5 mins)**
**See Page 18**
**Try to make some of your own relevant to whatever has happened during the session**

Section 5: Social Skills

Session 3

# THE BAG GAME

**A selection of pictures of sports:**

Hockey
Football
Basketball
Tennis
Rugby
Cricket
Swimming

---

Section 5: Social Skills

Session 2

# SWEETS

---

Section 5: Social Skills

Session 3

# WHAT MAKES A GOOD FRIEND?

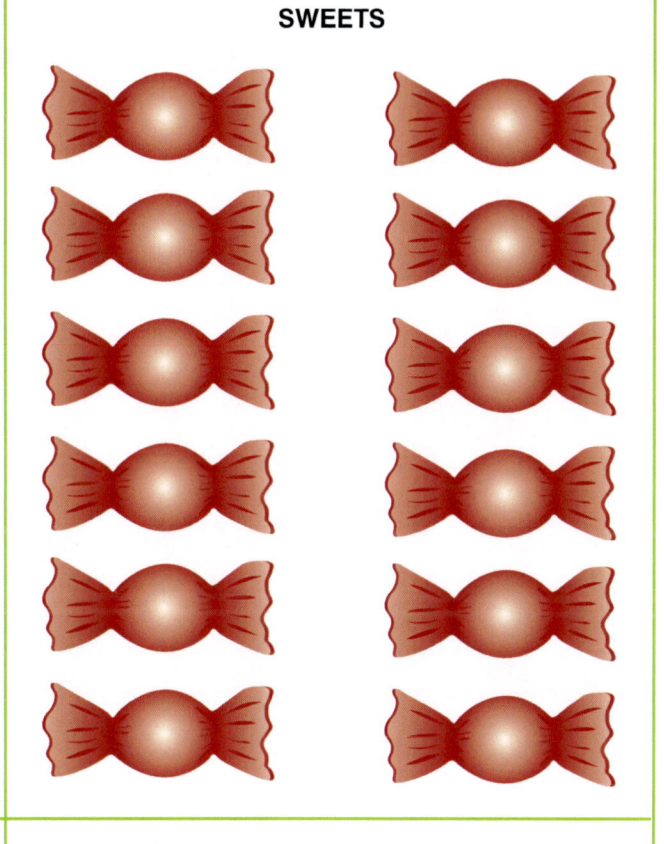

---

Section 5: Social Skills

Session 3

# ROLE PLAY CARDS

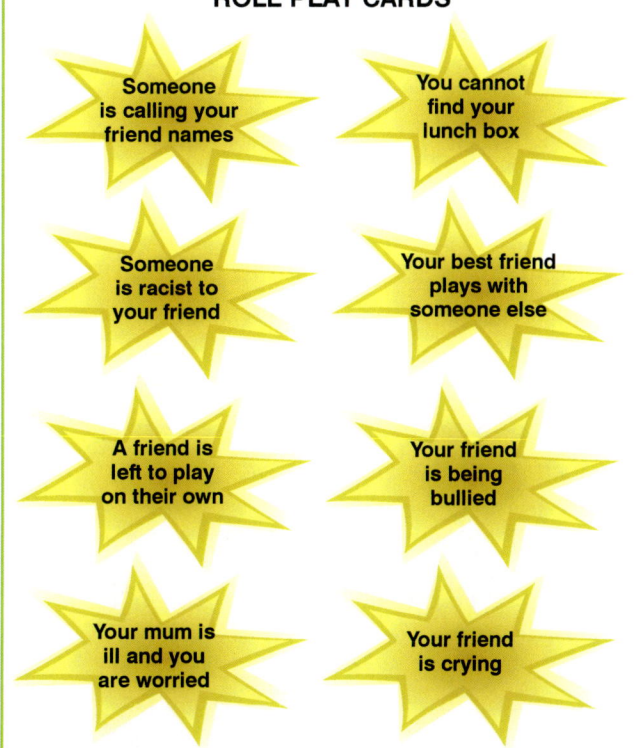

- Someone is calling your friend names
- You cannot find your lunch box
- Someone is racist to your friend
- Your best friend plays with someone else
- A friend is left to play on their own
- Your friend is being bullied
- Your mum is ill and you are worried
- Your friend is crying

Copyright of the Nurture Group Network 2011

# Section 5: Social Skills
# Session 4
# Introduction

The facilitator can once again reinforce the group rules prior to engaging the students in 'Taking Turns' Circle game. This involves going around the circle in turns. The facilitator introduces the activity by asking the students the question 'When do we take turns in school?' A short 'thinking' time should then be provided. The facilitator can then begin the sentence completion activity: 'At school I take turns when....., 'This then becomes a 'round' and each student must add to it as it comes to them.

This activity it is intended to reinforce turn taking, memorising, listening to others, understanding how others memorise things differently etc.

## The Bag Game

A bigger bag will be needed for this activity. The bag will be placed in the centre of the circle and will be filled with well known games, e.g. a pack of playing cards, Uno, snakes and ladders, chess, etc. The students should name the game and say something about the game, talking for up to 30 secs each. The facilitator can emphasise the importance of taking turns in games

## Activities
## Favourite Games Activity

The facilitator can ask the students: 'What is your favourite game?' The students will be given time out to plan a talk about their favourite game. Each student will be given 1 minute (timed on a sand-timer) to give a talk to the other students. They can then reflect on how they felt as they gave their talk and all students can evaluate each talk identifying what was of interest and what detail may have added more to the description.

## Favourite Games – How to Play Activity.

The facilitator can explain that each student will next create an activity sheet explaining how to play their favourite game. The facilitator can ask questions such as: What would you need to play the game? What are the rules? What does your game look like?
Each student can then complete a 'How to Play...' activity sheet. It may be helpful for students to pair up in order to discuss this activity and to check out with each other how useful and accurate their descriptions are.

## Always finish with Closing Compliments (5 mins)
## See Page 18
## Try to make some of your own relevant to whatever has happened during the session

**Section 5: Social Skills**

**Session 4**

## THE BAG GAME
### (Larger bag needed)

**A selection of games:**

Playing cards
Uno
Snakes and Ladders
Chess
Connect four etc

**Section 5: Social Skills**

**Session 4**

## HOW TO PLAY

**You will need:**

**Rules:**

**This is what my game looks like:**

# Section 5: Social Skills
# Session 5
# Introduction

The facilitator can reinforce the group rules prior to engaging the students in 'Who am I?' circle game. This involves going around the circle in turns. The facilitator introduces the activity by asking the students to study every student in the circle carefully. This will involve looking at colour of eyes, colour of hair, shape of nose etc.' Each student must think of 4/5 statements about the appearance/features of the student they have chosen. They can then take it in turns so that each student can make 4/5 statements about the student and the other students are then asked to guess who they are describing.

This activity it is intended as a reinforcement of turn taking skills, observing, listening to others, etc.

## The Bag Game

The bag is once again passed around the circle containing a selection of cards that depict different facial expressions. Students take turns to select a face and describe it, including what mood they think the face is showing. The facilitator can once again emphasise the importance of taking turns and listening to others and then ask students if they can make the expressions?

## Activities
## Share Your Problem Activity

The facilitator will ask the student s to, show a listening face. He/She can start a discussion by asking about problems that people might have, e.g. being bullied, a stomachache, finding it difficult to make friends etc. The facilitator will ask: Can you be a good friend who listens to problems? Can you talk to a friend because you know they will be good at helping?

The facilitator can next give each student a 'Talk to Me' activity sheet and a "problem". Students will be given a few minutes to prepare and then they will be put into pairs and asked to 'interview' each other.

The rest of the group can observe the interviews and evaluate each other's performance.

**Always finish with Closing Compliments (5 mins)
See Page 18
Try to make some of your own relevant to whatever has happened during the session**

Section 5: Social Skills

Session 5

# THE BAG GAME

**A selection of cards showing different expressions:**

Smiling
Angry
Confused
Sad
Scared
Excited

---

Section 5: Social Skills

Session 5

# TALK TO ME
Share your problems!!! Tell a friend!!

**Interview each other using the questions.
Find the best solution to the problem.**
1. What is the problem?
2. How do you feel?
3. What would you like to happen?
4. What do you need to do to change it?
5. What can you do differently?

**Draw a solution**

---

Section 5: Social Skills

Session 5

# TALK TO ME

**Draw some pictures that show different ways to help your friends with problems. What can you do??**

# Section 5: Social Skills
# Session 6
# Introduction

The facilitator can begin by asking the question: 'What music calms you? This involves going around the circle and asking each person to continue in turn. The facilitator then introduces the activity as a 'round': The music that calms me is....e.g. quiet, soft, etc. The students will then discuss the differences in responses.

This activity it is intended to reinforce the skills of turn taking, listening to others, understanding that we all have different needs when we want to calm and different preferences for the methods that we employ to do this.

## The Bag Game

The bag is once again passed around the circle containing a selection of numbers. The student can take turns to select a number. This number will then be played on the selected CD which the facilitator will have prepared prior to the start of the session. Each student will talk about how the selected tune made them feel.

## Listen up Activity

The facilitator will next play different types of music to the students. The students will be encouraged to discuss how they felt after the first two pieces of music.

The facilitator can play a further selection of different types of music and there will be an activity sheet for the students to fill in after each piece of music in order to describe their resulting feelings.

Students can then identify the similarities and differences in their feeling and responses to the music.

## Making an Album

The facilitator can then ask the students to select the pieces of music that made them feel calm from the last activity. Each piece of music that they chose will be played and further discussed.
The facilitator and the students can then compile an album together on a CD.
The CD can be played as the students evaluate each piece of music.
The facilitator can ask the students to create an album with a sleeve to list their songs.

**Always finish with Closing Compliments (5 mins)
See Page 18
Try to make some of your own relevant to whatever has happened during the session**

Section 5: Social Skills

Session 6

## THE BAG GAME

**Cards with numbers:**

(Numbers will depend on how many tracks on the selected CD)

---

Section 5: Social Skills

Session 6

## CREATE AN ALBUM COVER FOR YOUR CD

---

Section 5: Social Skills

Session 6

## MAKE A TRACK LIST FOR YOUR ALBUM COVER

1.

2.

3.

4.

5.

# Section 5 Social Skills
# Session 7
# Introduction

The facilitator begins by reinforcing the group rules and then explaining the rules of the first game. One student stands in the middle of the circle blindfolded. The other children pass something noisy (a bunch of keys) around the circle. When the pupil in the middle thinks they know where the 'keys' are they shout 'stop' and point in the direction. If they are correct they swap places with that person. If they not correct the 'keys' are passed around again. When the facilitator stops the game s/he asks the students 'what made this activity difficult'? and 'how did they overcome these difficulties'. The idea here is to focus on the importance of good listening and developing our skills in this area

## The Bag Game

The bag is passed around the circle containing a selection of disability aids or pictures of these, e.g. hearing aid, picture of a wheelchair, picture of a white stick, picture of a guide dog etc. Each student will either talk about why their aid is needed or ask for help and another student will volunteer to help by explaining why the aid is needed. The facilitator will then finish the activity by asking each student how they think they would manage if they had the disability related to the aid they are holding.

## Using your eyes

The facilitator will begin to mime sentences to the students with her/his mouth and watch for the reaction.

The facilitator can then explain that the students will need to use their eyes for this activity. Each student will be given a clipboard, and pen with the recording activity sheet. All students will need to be close enough to the facilitator see her/his mouth. The facilitator will mouth 10 questions, e.g. What is your name? How old are you? Which football team do you support? etc. Each student will have to write the answer to each question. If they can't they will leave a blank on their piece of paper.

The facilitator can ask the students how easy/difficult the task was and why? The facilitator will then say each question out loud and the students will check their answers.

The group can then discuss difficulties experienced if someone is deaf or hearing impaired.

**Always finish with Closing Compliments (5 mins)**
**See Page 18**
**Try to make some of your own relevant to whatever has happened during the session**

**Section 5: Social Skills**

**Session 7**

## THE BAG GAME

**Cards with pictures of:**

A wheelchair
A white stick
A guide dog
A hearing aid
Glasses
Prosthetic limb

**Section 5: Social Skills**

**Session 8**

## USING YOUR EYES - RECORDING SHEET

| | |
|---|---|
| **1.** | |
| **2.** | |
| **3.** | |
| **4.** | |
| **5.** | |
| **6.** | |
| **7.** | |
| **8.** | |
| **9.** | |
| **10.** | |

# Section 5: Social Skills
# Session 8
# Introduction

The facilitator will reinforce the group rules and then tell the students that they are going to play a game and that they will have a selection of small classroom items on a tray that are used regularly in the class. The students will be told that they are going to memorise the objects by looking at them for 1-2 minutes.

The facilitator can then hide the objects and then take 2 of them away ensuring that the students are unable to view this process. The tray will then be brought back into full view and the students will work in pairs and try and work out which items are missing. They can then discuss how they worked out which were missing and check out if they were right or not. The game can be repeated as many times as the students/facilitator wishes.

# The Bag Game

The bag is once again passed around the circle containing a selection of the items from 'Kim's Game' (as described above). Students can take turns to select an item. Each student will tell the other students how they remembered the item or items that had been removed or selected during 'Kim's Game'.

# Activity
# Listening

The facilitator can discuss with the class the following questions; How do people know we are listening to them? Where can we go in school to talk and listen? Who would they chose to talk to? What can we say or do so someone knows we want to listen to them but don't have time at that moment? The facilitator record their ideas on the white board as the students say them.

# Talk to Me

The facilitator can then look at and discuss the worksheets with the group of students and consider how they can engage in role play. The facilitator can then place the students into pairs and tell them to swap their activity sheets when finished (adult help will be needed for non readers).

The students may then complete activity sheet.

The facilitator may wish to leave the ideas on the board in order to prompt the students to label their work.

# Always finish with Closing Compliments (5 mins)
# See Page 18
# Try to make some of your own relevant to whatever has happened during the session

Section 5: Social Skills

Session 8

## THE BAG GAME

**Small objects used daily from around the classroom:**

---

Section 5: Social Skills

Session 8

## TALK TO ME
Share your problems!!! Tell a friend!!

**Interview each other using the questions.
Find the best solution to the problem.**
1. What is the problem?
2. How do you feel?
3. What would you like to happen?
4. What do you need to do to change it?
5. What can you do differently?

**Draw a solution**

---

Section 5: Social Skills

Session 8

## TALK TO ME

**Draw some pictures that show different ways to help your friends with problems. What can you do??**

# Section 5: Social Skills
# Session 9
# Introduction

The facilitator can reinforce the group rules and then remind the students of Kim's Game from Session 8. This will be reinforced by playing the game once or twice to strengthen their knowledge of the game.

The facilitator can then split the group into 2s or 3s and provide them with a Kim's game for each group. The students will be told that they need to follow the same rules but they must organise between them who will take on which role. The facilitator can monitor how they organise the game and step in and bring the group together when necessary.

Students can then discuss how they worked out who would take each role, identifying any disagreements and/or who was helpful and took a leadership role and why.

## The Bag Game

The bag is once again passed around the circle containing a selection of the items from each of the groups' 'Kim's Game'. Students can take turns to select an item. Each student will study the item and then take turns to point out specific memorable features to enable them to remember them. The items will then be hidden and one student at a time will be selected to remember every item.

## Activity
## Friendship Games: Blindfolded Obstacle Course

This game promotes both trust and listening. Students are paired in groups of two: one plays the guide, the other the blindfolded student. Once groups are established, the groups will race against each other though an obstacle course. The blindfolded student must navigate the course by following the commands of his/her partner. The guide gives commands like, "Left," "Right" or "Straight," along with warning the blind partner about upcoming obstacles. To make sure both students get equal exposure, the facilitator will make the game a two-way race. Once the first blindfolded student has reached the end of the obstacle course, s/he switches positions with the guide and then guides his/her friend back over the course. The first team to complete a two-way journey wins.

The game can then be discussed and evaluated. Students can discuss what made a good team and how important it is to work together.

## Human Knot

The facilitator can explain that this game involves the cooperation of the entire group. All students will stand in a circle and grab the hand of someone in the circle, but it cannot be the person to their right or left. Once everyone has grabbed hands, they must untangle themselves without letting go of their companion's hands. The students must communicate and plan how they are going to break the knot. Some of the players may end facing outward, which is okay, as long as no one lets go. No activity sheet required for this session.

**Always finish with Closing Compliments (5 mins)**
**See Page 18  Try to make some of your own relevant to whatever has happened during the session**

**Section 5: Social Skills**

**Session 9**

## THE BAG GAME

**Small objects used daily from around the classroom that have been used in session 9's Kim's Game:**

# Section 5: Social Skills
# Session 10
# Introduction

The facilitator will reinforce group rules and then explain that the " I am your friend" game which encourages students to learn to recognise their friends' voices. The students sit together in a semi circle. One student is chosen to be 'it' and sits in the chair with his/her back to the group, with eyes closed or with a blindfold. A student is chosen by the facilitator from the group. S/he tiptoes up to the chair, taps the student sitting in the chair on the back, and in a disguised or funny voice says, "Do you know me? I'm your friend." The mystery student then rejoins the group and the guessing begins! The student in the chair uncovers his/her eyes, turns around, and tries to guess the name of the 'friend' who tapped and talked. After three guesses, a new student takes the chair and gets a turn

## The Bag Game

The bag is once again passed around the circle containing a selection of friendship traits/behaviours (recorded on cards) from the 'table' below e.g. caring, sharing, listening. Students take turns to select one from the bag. Each student will study what they have selected and then take turns to point act out/mime/describe without using the word or phrase. The other students will try and guess the behaviour or trait.

## Activity
## A Good Friend Should Be...

The facilitator can then ask the group 'What makes a good friend?' All the suggestions can be written down on the whiteboard and discussed.
The students will then work in pairs and complete an activity sheet together discussing each suggestion before writing 'true' or 'false'.

## Friendship Chain

The facilitator can provide each student with strips of coloured card. Each student can be instructed to decorate and write the name of a friend on one of the strips. The facilitator can encourage students to take turns adding their strips to the chain. The chain can be displayed in the classroom.

The students can then repeat the process but this time each student will write a good trait of a friend.

The facilitator can keep a supply of card strips near the display and invite the students to continue adding strips to the class friendship chain whenever they feel they need to.

## Always finish with Closing Compliments (5 mins)
## See Page 18
## Try to make some of your own relevant to whatever has happened during the session

Section 5: Social Skills

Session 10

# THE BAG GAME

A selection of friendship traits from the table below:

---

Section 5: Social Skills

Session 10

| Caring | Share | Demand too much | Energetic |
| Respectful | Take turns | Dishonest | Excitement |
| Patient | Have fun together | Bully | Secure |
| Understanding | Listen | Talk too much | Happiness |
| Trustworthy | Act Nicely | Deceitful | Confident |

---

Section 5: Social Skills

Session 10

## A GOOD FRIEND SHOULD:

Names _____ and _____

| Quality | True | False |
|---|---|---|
| • Be honest | | |
| • Live in a big house | | |
| • Be a good listener | | |
| • Do whatever I say | | |
| • Have lots of toys and games | | |
| • Wear nice clothes | | |
| • Be kind | | |
| • Only talk to me | | |
| • Have other friends | | |
| • Be forgiving | | |
| • Be interested in other people | | |
| • Have lots of money | | |
| • Care about other people | | |
| • Do the right thing | | |
| • Always agree with what I say | | |
| • Bring me presents all the time | | |
| • | | |
| • | | |

# Part 3 - Appendices

- **Setting Up The Grange Nurture Group – A history in words and pictures**

- **Case Studies**

- **The Pre and Post Skills Checklist**

- **Information Sheet for Staff and Parents**

# Setting Up the Grange Nurture Group – A History in Words and Pictures

This is a record of how we set up our Nurture Base in words and pictures. This diary will illustrate the physical set up and the way in which we developed specific areas to address the social and emotional learning needs of our students.

The room that was originally the residential playroom has been totally refurbished with all original fixtures and fittings removed. We have had all walls painted in calming pastel colours and the room is now available for dining at lunch time and activities during class times. It is now spacious and flexible and can be used for whatever purpose may be required by the facilitators. The residential sitting room in the house looked like a drab waiting room. Again we have removed all original fixtures and fittings for a massive transformation. The walls have been painted in calm pastel colours. A purpose built bench has been constructed with storage space within it. This area is now our soft room available for all students at The Grange but mainly the Nurture Group. The students can access this room to calm and the facilitator can use this area for many of the activities. Everything is soft and easily accessible the television is mounted on the wall out of the way.

The room that we chose for our main Nurture Classroom was used for residential purposes in the evenings. It was very dated and cold; therefore all original fixtures and fittings were removed. It was painted in calming pastel colours it was then furnished with small plastic tables and chairs that are easily moved around the classroom. Bright rugs were placed on the floors with areas purpose built for reading, role-play, listening and quiet area, sand and water areas, and learning. The purpose of this room is to provide an inviting and nurturing environment for students who need the nurturing atmosphere to help develop their social, emotional and behavioural skills.

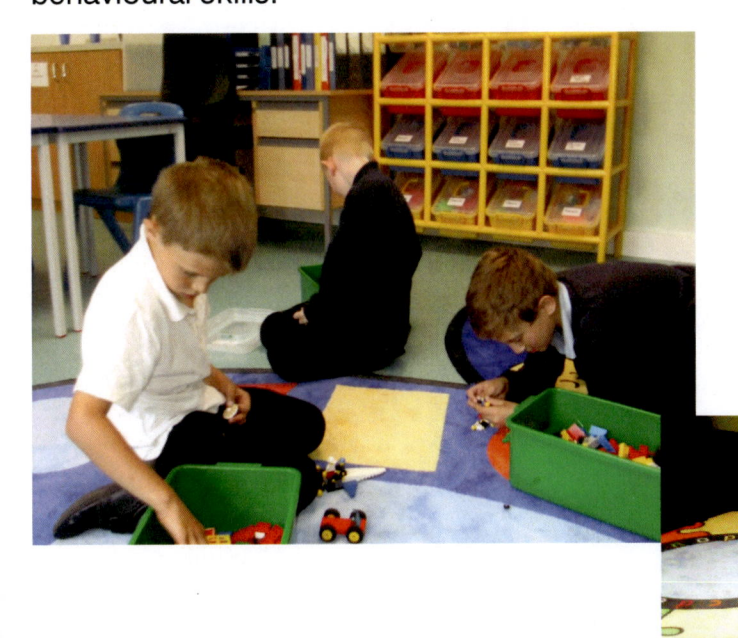

# The main Nurture Classroom before the refurbishment

This was the residential students' main playroom. It is a large room so we felt that it was ideal for the main nurture classroom.

This was the room that we spent most time planning and designing. We wanted it to accommodate all the different areas for each domain.

It was completely gutted and refurbished. New storage cupboards were fitted. The room already had a sink so we decided a 'student level' sink along with an adult sink should be fitted so that the students could be responsible for cleaning up after 'messy play'.

# Pictures before the refurbishment

This was originally used as a second playroom for the residential students in the evening. During the day it was used for 1-1 sessions with the learning support teacher but it was not ideal because there were many distractions. It also became a 'dumping ground' for resources because of the lack of space. This is a large room and will be ideal for activities such as dance therapy. It will also double up as the lunch time dining room.

This was the residential sitting room. The furniture had been removed when the students moved to another house and it began to look like a waiting room. This will be ideal for the 'soft' room where the students will be withdrawn for quiet time or when they need to release their aggressive feelings.

This was the residential students' 'boot room'. This will be ideal for the cloakroom where students will have their named pegs and cupboards where they will be responsible for their own belongings.

# Work in Progress

**Before Refurbishment**

**During Refurbishment**

A purpose built storage bench was built around the fireplace. This was for safety reasons as well as aesthetic and storage needs. This will have fitted soft seats and a fitted soft back to stay in keeping with the idea of the 'soft' room.

**Before Refurbishment**

**During Refurbishment**

Purpose built storage cupboards were fitted throughout the new dining/activity room to house the many new nurture resources as well as the curriculum resources for Lower School.

# Case Studies

Frank
Damien
Simon

## Case Study 1 - Background

Frank joined the school aged 8 years old. He had been excluded from the mainstream sector because of his unacceptable behaviour and had been in a Pupil Referral Unit prior to attending The Grange.

Frank lived with his mother and 2 younger sisters. He had sporadic contact with his father. A social work report noted that there were no rules or boundaries in the home. The children put themselves to bed and fed themselves when they were hungry.

Frank had been referred to a Speech and Language Therapist because he has a speech impediment. He is unable to pronounce some sounds and mispronounces other sounds.

Frank turned up to school each morning looking unkempt. He had felt pen marks on his hands from the previous day and had ground in dirt in his nails. Frank had nits and when a letter was sent home and a follow up phone call was made Frank came to school with a shaven head.

## Checklist Assessment Observations

Frank was observed as a feral child. He knew no boundaries or rules and resisted any encouragement to sit at a table or sit on a chair.

When given free range of the nurture room Frank would find paper and felt pens and would draw and colour quietly by himself. There was no positive interaction with other children. If another child came near to where he was standing (he didn't sit to colour) he would lash out or tell them aggressively to 'Fuck off'. Frank frequently used racist and sexualised language seemingly unaware of what it meant. He spat at anyone who came too close to him and became very aggressive to the point of picking up chairs and attempting to throw them if he was interrupted in any way. Frank rarely joined in activities if he was asked to do so. He didn't know how to take turns or share. If he wanted something that another child was playing with he would take it and fight over it. If he approached a game where students were taking turns he would join in without asking and 'cheat' in order to win every time.

He rarely engaged in conversation and rarely maintained eye-contact, preferring his own company.

Frank was unable to listen to a story read by an adult. He appeared uninterested and wandered round the room unaware of what was expected of him.

When playing in the playground at break-times Frank often chose to play football but was unable to cope with the rules and would regularly start fights often with boys much older and bigger than himself appearing unaware of the consequences of his actions or his own safety. Improvements through the Nurture Group

Frank will now sit throughout most introductory circle sessions. He listens to others and understands how to take turns.

Frank will now sit when he is required to take part in writing tasks. He will always draw and colour pictures all over his work but he often asks for written work rather than hands on activities. He is becoming excited by his own learning.

Frank likes to have his own table when he works. He always places 2 chairs at his table and sits on both until an adult comes near and then he will move over and will invite the adult to sit with him. He then explains what he is doing. This shows a huge improvement in some areas of his social skills. Frank used to flinch if an adult came too close to him. He needed his own personal space where no one was invited or allowed. Frank will also ask the adults in the nurture room for 'hugs' during the day. This shows that Frank is secure in his surroundings.

Frank has been observed to 'help' another student when he was struggling with tasks, showing empathy. He is beginning to talk about his own feelings but this is still an area he finds difficult and will swear aggressively if he feels under pressure.

Frank still has very aggressive outbursts and will attack other students if they have upset him in any way. Frank was observed digging up a daisy plant in the grounds and excitedly showed adults. He then hid it to plant it later in his 'nurture' garden. Another older student then unwittingly damaged it. Frank was so distraught that he kicked and punched the older student and had to be removed by adults. This shows that Frank still needs nurturing in managing his own feelings.

Frank will now listen to a story read by an adult. He will often wander around and/or draw while it is read but he can then retell the story and will sequence pictures to show the correct order of the story.

## Case Study 2 - Background

Damien joined the school aged 8 years old. He had been excluded from the mainstream sector because of his unacceptable behaviour. He has long standing difficulties with emotional and behavioural development. He began receiving 1-1 support at his previous school due to his impulsive and unpredictable behaviour which often resulted in physical assaults on staff and children. Damien's speech and language skills are underdeveloped which in turn with his other difficulties means his social skills are lacking and nowhere near age appropriate. These delays have resulted in Damien not meeting developmental milestones; therefore we decided to put him forward as a candidate for our Nurture Group. Damien is being referred for further investigations and is in the process of being diagnosed with Autism although this isn't confirmed. As a result of having this information we decided to complete our checklist to see if he belonged in the Nurture Classroom.

## Checklist Assessment Observations

When Damien arrived we observed him in class and out of class and then were able to complete our 'pre-intervention checklist'. We found that Damien had little understanding of his own and others' feelings. He had no friendship skills, little comprehension of school behaviours and how to act in the social aspect of school having very little social skills. Looking at the results from our 'pre-intervention checklist' we discovered that Damien was a prime candidate for our nurture curriculum and classroom. This together with our observations painted the picture that Damien needed to go back to basics and start again. He had no concept of interacting with other children and didn't know how to behave or learn in a 'normal' classroom environment.

When given free reign of the Nurture Classroom Damien would often order building bricks or game pieces and create an army. He never chose to interact or play with other students, certainly not of a positive nature. If another student approached him or entered his 'army base' it would result in him lashing out and calling them naughty. If the other student persisted to 'annoy' him his protests would become louder until he would jump up and down and punch himself in the head while rambling inaudibly. When asked why he had hurt himself his response was always because they are naughty.

Damien was also observed to head butt anything that touched him in a negative way, for example; if he walked passed a door and didn't leave himself enough space and he knocked his arm he would head butt the door also if he fell over himself he would head butt the floor. When asked why he does this and asked not to hurt himself his response was, "If anything that doesn't belong to me touches me I head butt it, and that's the way it is"

Damien didn't use his seat and became increasingly distressed when asked to sit down to partake in classroom activities.

At break times Damien would chose to participate in make believe games about armies on his own and would only let other students play if he was in charge. If a student came and took over his game we would see similar behaviours to the classroom of jumping up and down etc.

## Improvements through the Nurture Group

In the short time that Damien has been following our programme he is already becoming more socially aware. He is now able to play simple games with other students, albeit for short periods of time. He is displaying less head butting (although it does still happen). Damien feels comfortable in his nurture surroundings and is now completing short activities at the end of sessions, although he still prefers not to sit down while he works.

Damien can still become distressed when asked to complete pen and paper activities but there are fewer of these behaviours. He enjoys the hands on learning that takes place in the Nurture Group and is interacting more positively with both students and staff. As a result of this he is more confident and more willing to learn.

We are happy with Damien's progress and believe that without the Nurture Group he would still display many of these concerning behaviours which could cause harm to both himself and others around him. We have completed our 'pre and post intervention checklist' (post intervention)and have discovered that Damien was scoring mostly 'nevers' in the feelings category and is now scoring 'occasionally' and 'sometimes'. This shows that he is becoming more aware of his and other people's feelings. Friendship skills have improved a little but not huge amounts. We can also see that his social skills have improved. The biggest achievement comes in the school behaviours section where he scored no 'nevers' at all this time compared to nearly all 'nevers' when we originally performed the checklist.

# Case Study 3 - Background

Simon joined us when he was 8 years old. Unfortunately it wasn't just his education that wasn't running smoothly it was also his home life. Simon was in foster care, awaiting his 2nd foster placement as his current one had broken down. Simon still had sporadic supervised parental visits. He has been known to Social Care for the majority of his childhood and has needed close supervision and clear boundaries most of his life to keep himself and others safe. Simon struggles to settle and comply with basic social conformities in and out of school, as a result of this there is a significant barrier to Simon's learning and he is academically delayed.

Despite only being 8 years old Simon's difficulties have been long standing and are not aided by the fact that both of his parents display significant learning difficulties themselves.

Simon has come to us from a Primary Pupil Referral Unit where he was placed from his large Primary School. His behaviours became too difficult to be supported there.

# Checklist Assessment Observations

When Simon arrived at the Grange we were able to observe him in and out of class to see where we would like to place him in the school. These observations allowed us to complete our 'pre and post-intervention checklist'. We discovered that Simon was lacking in all the areas defined by our checklist and had little or no feelings about himself or others around him and no friendship skills, as he didn't show any interest in others at all. He had no idea how to access classroom activities and he lacked appropriate school behaviours and as a result of all this Simon displayed no social skills.

The results of our checklist and our observations made us very aware that Simon needed to be placed within our Nurture Group, in order to help him build on these skills and be able to learn in a classroom environment.

When given free reign of the classroom Simon would often ask to play a card game with an adult and when encouraged to interact with other students became agitated and disruptive. When he did interact with other students it had to be under his terms he liked to be in charge. When Simon did interact with other students it never lasted long as the communication and fun of the game would soon break down. Simon also got distressed if people were on/near his desk as he was worried that they would touch or use his stuff.

Simon would sometimes listen very well to the delivery of sessions and sometimes wouldn't. When he didn't he would randomly scream words very loudly or begin to pick on another member of the class to gain a reaction and disrupt the session. After the effect when he was calm there was never any remorse, not even towards the student he had picked on.

The thing we observed most with Simon was there never seemed to be any triggers for his disruptive or violent behaviours. He could be sitting working and being praised for it and all of a sudden would become agitated or disruptive, and sometimes verbally abusive and violent. We were very concerned about these behaviours and were concerned that we place Simon in the correct group to help him socially, emotionally and educationally. After the observations and the completion of checklist we were sure that the correct place for him was our 'Nurture Group' as this would enable him the freedom and space to become used to a 'normal' learning environment again.

# Improvements through the Nurture Group

Since he has joined the Nurture Group we have seen improvements with Simon's behaviour and school work. Although these have been small improvements they are there and visual. Simon still displays very difficult and challenging behaviours but they are slightly more controlled now and he has learnt skills that enable him to socialise a little more with his peers. He is able to be part of games now for longer periods of time and isn't as concerned with being in charge any more. He can cooperate in group activities and is slightly better at waiting his turn (for short periods of time).

We decided for the purpose of this book to retake the checklist and analyse it for improvements. He has made improvements with his understanding of his own and others feelings as a result of the activities that he has taken part in in the Nurture Group. His friendship skills have also improved and he understands some concepts of being a friend although he still couldn't put all these skills together to sustain a friendship. His school behaviours have improved a little although his behaviour can still be erratic and unexplainable. Also his social skills have improved further as he is able to take part in group work and playing games. Although Simon has made improvements in the short time he has been in our Nurture Group he is going to benefit from being there longer to enable him to re-access a 'normal' classroom and learning environment.

# Pre-Intervention Checklist

## Please rate the pupil against each of the following statements, ticking the appropriate boxes

| Feelings | Always | Mainly | Sometimes | Occasionally | Never |
|---|---|---|---|---|---|
| Can recognise and label how they feel. | | | | | |
| Can recognise how others are feeling | | | | | |
| Can show empathy towards others. | | | | | |
| Can tell an adult when they feel distressed | | | | | |
| Can tell another peer when they feel distressed. | | | | | |
| Can distinguish between comfortable and uncomfortable feelings accurately. | | | | | |
| Has appropriate emotional vocabulary to express feelings accurately. | | | | | |
| Can express anger without physical aggression. | | | | | |
| **Friendship Skills** | | | | | |
| Shows interest in other pupils. | | | | | |
| Can approach a peer and ask to play with them. | | | | | |
| Understands the concept of kindness. | | | | | |
| Understands the concept of sharing. | | | | | |
| Understands the concept of turn-taking. | | | | | |
| Can identify one or more friends in class. | | | | | |
| Can identify one of more friends at home. | | | | | |
| Will apologise to a friend when necessary. | | | | | |
| Will help out a friend when necessary. | | | | | |
| Has shown the ability to sustain a friendship. | | | | | |

| School Behaviours | Always | Mainly | Sometimes | Occasionally | Never |
|---|---|---|---|---|---|
| Looks at the adult when called. | | | | | |
| Looks at another child when called. | | | | | |
| Can maintain eye-contact when talking. | | | | | |
| Does not interrupt the speaker. | | | | | |
| Waits for a turn to talk. | | | | | |
| Understands what is being said. | | | | | |
| Follows instructions appropriately. | | | | | |
| Uses appropriate volume when speaking. | | | | | |
| Uses the appropriate vocabulary to express needs, wants and ideas. | | | | | |
| Can sit appropriately to listen to a story or teacher instructions. | | | | | |
| Can concentrate on an activity without interrupting others. | | | | | |
| Knows what is 'safe' to do in class. | | | | | |
| Knows what is 'unsafe' to do in class. | | | | | |
| Knows how to play and interact safely in the playground. | | | | | |
| Knows when behaviour is unsafe in the playground | | | | | |
| Follows classroom routines and rules to keep safe. | | | | | |
| Follows playground routines and rules to keep safe. | | | | | |

| Social Skills | Always | Mainly | Sometimes | Occasionally | Never |
|---|---|---|---|---|---|
| Can take turns appropriately in conversation. | | | | | |
| Can take turns appropriately in a game. | | | | | |
| Plays well with one other pupil in a game or turn-taking activity. | | | | | |
| Knows what is 'safe' to do in class. | | | | | |
| Knows what is 'unsafe' to do in class. | | | | | |
| Knows how to play and interact safely in the playground. | | | | | |
| Knows when behaviour is unsafe in the playground. | | | | | |
| Follows classroom routines and rules to keep safe. | | | | | |
| Follows playground routines and rules to keep safe. | | | | | |
| Can work well alongside one other pupil on a class based learning task. | | | | | |
| Can participate well in a group activity: helping, turn-taking, supporting others in need. | | | | | |
| Cooperates with peers and plays effectively in the playground. | | | | | |

# Information Sheet for Staff and Parents

This information sheet aims to describe the nurture group approach and philosophy and to briefly outline the curriculum offered to the target students.

## Introduction

Nurture groups were developed in 1969 in inner London. They were developed in response to the large number of children presenting to psychological services with severe social, emotional and behavioural problems on entry to school. Marjorie Boxall, an educational psychologist, recognised these difficulties and the fact that they were generally the outcome of impoverished early nurturing. This had resulted in many of the young children being unable to make trusting relationships with adults and also having significant difficulties and responding appropriately to other children. In effect, they were deemed not to be ready to meet the social and intellectual demands of school life.

## So what is the aim of the nurture group?

- For Boxall it was to create the world of earliest childhood building the basic and essential learning experiences normally gained in the first three years of life and enable children to fully meet their potential in mainstream schools.

## What is a nurture group?

- It is an inclusive early intervention and prevention of social and emotional difficulties within a school based setting.
- It is a provision in which the day is one of carefully structured routines which provide a balance of learning and teaching, affection and structure within a home like environment.
- It is a group in which young children and students are placed; not because of limitations in cognitive ability but because they have clearly missed out upon early experiences that promote good development.

It is important to remember that nurture groups can be accessed by younger children and students across the key stages. Young people who display such behaviours and have clearly not had the opportunity to form secure attachments in their early years can all benefit from this type of provision regardless of their age.

## Characteristics of Nurture Groups

Nurture groups have a number of characteristics which are evident in practice. These were developed by the Nurture Group Network. Nurture groups offer a context and model of relationships for children who have been missing, or have insufficiently internalised essential early learning experiences. They are a within school resource staffed by two adults for up to 10 young people. Nurture groups offer short or medium term placements where the students attend regularly usually returning fully to their mainstream or special class context within 2-4 terms. The nurture groups do not stigmatise children who attend since the intervention is part of a whole school approach to supporting children. It is anticipated that students will maintain strong links with their mainstream or special class, for example registering there in the morning, attending selected activities and spending both break times and lunchtimes with their class peers.

The nurture room aims to provide a secure and predictable environment to meet the different needs of each student. There is always a strong focus on supporting positive, emotional and social growth and cognitive development at the level of the individual student by responding to each student in a developmentally appropriate way.

## What are the Principles?

### The nurture group should:

- Ensure the national curriculum is taught.
- Emphasise communication and language development through intensive interaction with an adult or other students.
- Provide opportunities for social learning through co-operation and play with others in a group with an appropriate mix of young people.
- Recognise the importance of quality play experiences in the development of children's learning.

The six guiding principles of nurture groups are as follows:

1. Children's learning is understood developmentally
2. The nurture group class offers a secure base
3. Nurture is important for self-esteem
4. Language is a vital means of communication
5. All behaviour is communication.
6. Transition is important in children's lives

### Key Features of a Nurture Group Room

In general, a nurture group room will consist of the following areas:

- Kitchen area
- Soft seating
- Dining area
- Role play area
- Work area

## How are Young People Assessed?

In order to gain access to a nurture group young people are identified on the basis of systematic assessment in which appropriate diagnostic and evaluative instruments have been used. The aim is always to return the young person to full-time mainstream or special provision as appropriate. The Boxall Profile provides the framework for the structured observation of young people in the classroom and consists of two sections: developmental profile and diagnostic profile. The profile was developed as part of the nurture group approach to allow a precise way of assessing areas of difficulty that young people experience in order to enable a focused and planned intervention and also a way of measuring progress. In our nurture group the Boxall Profile is utilised in conjunction with our own pre and post skills checklist. This is designed to highlight the social and emotional skills focused in our programme and to enable a more precise way of measuring areas for further development and focus.

# The Timetable

The majority of traditional nurture group sessions are likely to be approximately two hours in length and it is clearly more practical, in terms of the school timetable, to ensure that times remain consistent throughout the year. The first half hour of the session is when the children engage in free play; they can access a range of activities at this time and it is an ideal opportunity for staff to observe the children's learning and development of social and emotional skills. Table top and floor activities can be set up to cover each area of learning. The second 45 minutes of the session is when the children engage in group time. One member of the staff will lead the group whilst the other becomes a member of the group providing a role model for the children. Activities in this session may include the following:

- days of the week
- weather
- finding name cards
- choosing a special helper
- playing a short game linked to social skills development
- playing the 'bag' game

The next 30 minutes is for snack time. This is when a special helper helps prepare and serve the snack and drinks to the peer group. During this time both the adults and the children sit down together at the table; this enables the adults to model social conversation and engage in any problem solving regarding a current issue that may have arisen within the group. The next part of the session involves focused teaching. This is when one member of staff will carry out focused teaching tasks with individual children. Each child will try to complete the task during this time, either in a one to one or a small group context. This enables the other member of staff to interact with other children in their play whilst these activities are being implemented. The final part of the nurture group session is that of story time where one member of the staff reads a story to the group as a whole while the other member of staff becomes part of the group once again. This enables them to model appropriate behaviour, listening skills etc and also support the children's enjoyment, learning and development of language skills.

# Supporting Progress via the Social and Emotional Skills Programme

In our nurture group we also provide access to daily sessions of social and emotional skills based training. The programme we have designed is structured into five parts which are stored under the five SEAL headings as follows:

- Self-awareness
- Managing feelings
- Motivation
- Empathy
- Social skills

These practical and fun sessions aim to promote the development of social and emotional skills via a range of games and activities.

## Aims of the Approach

The aims of the approach are as follows:

- To enable students to develop the basic skills of communication e.g. appropriate looking, listening, conversation and turn taking skills.
- To enable students to develop a vocabulary for basic emotions and to identify and gain an understanding of these feelings that we all regularly experience.
- To enable students to define a friend and to be able to make and sustain friendships.
- To model genuine and appropriate social and emotional responses for students.
- To enable students to feel valued and nurtured.
- To improve students' self-concept.
- To promote self-respect and respect for others differences and values.
- To encourage students to be reflective and to monitor and evaluate the development of their own skills.
- To enable students to identify and distinguish between appropriate and inappropriate social behaviours in a range of contexts.
- To reinforce appropriate and safe 'play' skills in a range of contexts.

The extent to which these aims are met, will perhaps indicate the success or otherwise of the approach and its delivery.

## Conclusion

Nurture groups tend to work most effectively within schools which adopt a whole school approach to social inclusion and attempt to ensure the well-being of all staff and young people within their context. School staff who recognise and value the need and importance of building positive relationships tend to be most effective in developing and maintaining nurturing principles and successfully implementing this kind of intervention.

Overall, nurture groups can be very effective in building the resilience and confidence of young people who may be finding it difficult to cope in the classroom context. Nurture groups positively influence young people's lives particularly when access is provided at the earliest possible stage. The intensive support helps young people to flourish and grow and parents and carers need to be centrally involved in the nurture group programme in order to also reinforce skills and support their child's development in the home context.

The nurture group initiative adds an important dimension to the education of some of our most vulnerable young people. The approach needs to be flexible and creative and always underpinned by a nurturing philosophy. This then ensures that young people experience a sense of success which has a positive knock on effect in terms of their confidence, self-esteem and ability to learn. Young people in nurture groups will develop a growing sense of achievement and increase levels of motivation which can support their move back into the mainstream or specialist classroom context. This strong emphasis in nurture groups on developing children's language communication skills also helps to build a platform for further success.

We hope that this information sheet goes someway to describing the nature of the nurture group approach and also the underlying philosophy and basis in psychology. Overall, this kind of intervention aims to ensure the well-being and inclusion of all our young people within an inclusive school environment which recognises the importance of secure attachments and positive relationships between staff and students and the students themselves.

# The nurture group network
*helping children and young people to succeed*

## Nurturing Social and Emotional Development

**Nurturing Social and Emotional Development**

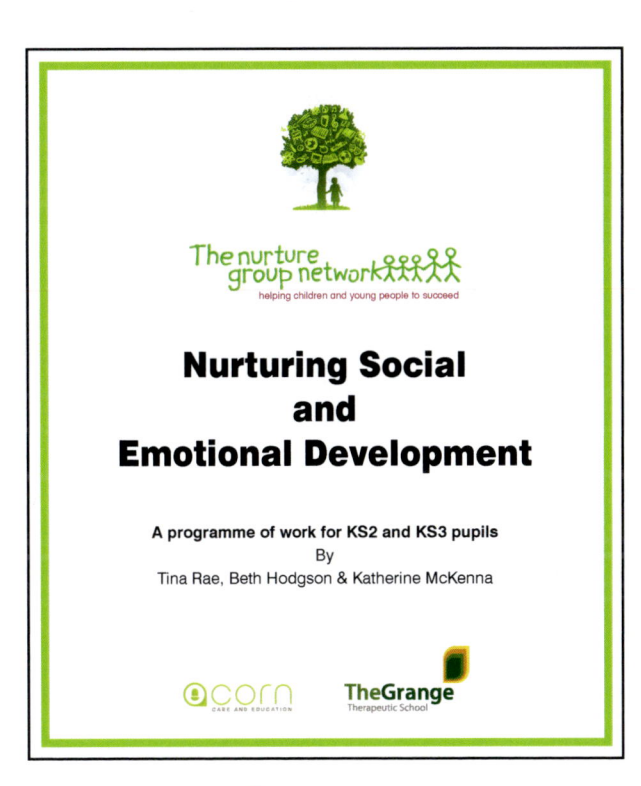

A programme of work for KS2 and KS3 pupils
By
Tina Rae, Beth Hodgson & Katherine McKenna

### Includes:

- **Worksheets**
- **Lesson Plans**
- **Cd**
- **Dvd**
- **Checklists**

## How to Order

| Publication | Qty | £10 P&P | Total |
|---|---|---|---|
| NURTURING SOCIAL AND EMOTIONAL DEVELOPMENT<br>Members - £65  Non Members - £75 | | | |

Postal / Invoice Address:
_____
_____
_____

E-mail Address _____

Tel: _____

Fax: _____

Please State: Member Yes / No

Membership No: _____

The Nurture Group Network
14 Beecham Court
Smithy Brook Road
Wigan
WN3 6PR
Tel: 01942 316085
Fax: 01942 568327
E-mail: lynne@nurturegroups.org

Please note this publication is despatched direct from our supplier Bamford Print via a National Courier company and will require a signature on receipt.